D1562000

Curses:

What They Are and How to Break Them

By
Dick Bernal

Companion Press
P.O. Box 351
Shippensburg, PA 17257-0351

ISBN 1-56043-468-6

For Worldwide Distribution

Printed in the U.S.A.

Foreword

As I read the manuscript of Dick Bernal's latest book, "Curses: What They Are and How to Break Them," I knew in my heart that the revelation contained in this work would truly set the captives free.

The book in its entirety is birthed out of two divine strains—the first strain being the immutable Word of God. Undeniably Dick's premises are grounded in the change-less Word of God. The revelation on deliverance from curses, without a doubt, has been a mystery and a hidden thing to most of the Body of Christ. The Bible clearly says: "The god of this world hath blinded the minds of those who do not believe." But Dick, by careful exegesis of the scripture, has taken the scales away from our eyes. Now with open eyes we can behold our Lord in greater dimensions than ever before.

The second strain is the crucible of human experience. Dick Bernal does not write this book from the perspective of a theological onlooker but as a man who himself had been bound and cursed until by divine revelation he was set free. I found myself praying as I read this manuscript that this book would become a best seller. I prayed this prayer for one reason—because I know that the Holy Spirit will massively use the revelation of this teaching in the hearts and lives of all who receive it.

Knowing Dick and Carla personally, I can gladly recommend the fruit of their lives as an epistle to be read by the whole Body of Christ—that revelational knowledge on deliverance from curses is real and powerful. Out of Dick's spiritual loins has been birthed the wonderful, multi-thousand member Jubilee Christian Center that is further testimony of the importance of this teaching. That which has been hidden from you is about to be revealed. As you read the next few pages, expect to encounter God and don't be surprised at the liberty He longs to give you.

In Christ,
Larry Lea

Table of Contents

Introduction

Curses and cursing are real! They are not reserved simply for remote heathen areas where witchcraft and superstition flourish. As a pastor and traveling minister, I am becoming increasingly aware that some people need more than healing. Many people leave a service cured and feeling touched by God's presence and power, but after a few days their problem returns—sometimes in worse form.

I am also discovering that deliverance isn't always enough. Demons may leave at the command and the name of Jesus but soon return with other evil entities to further torment the poor host.

What brings sickness and evil spirits back? Lack of faith? No real commitment? Sin in one's life? These can certainly create serious problems for the believer, but there is an area overlooked by most that I want to address in this book.

Many people are living under a curse. It might be a placed curse, a generational family curse, or a self-invoked curse. These and others we will deal with in some detail, answering such questions as:

- What is a curse?
- What are the symptoms?
- How can I discern the difference between a curse and other problems?
- And, how do I break a curse that is on me, my family, my friends or anyone the Lord leads across my path?

Get ready for a new and powerful dimension of ministry!

Like a flitting sparrow, like a flying swallow, So a curse without cause shall not alight.

Proverbs 26:2

Chapter 1

A Matter of Life or Death

What is wrong with me? I asked myself for the umpteenth time. Since returning from India some six months before, I had been listless, irritable and uncommonly depressed. At the urging of my wife Carla, I finally visited a doctor to see if perhaps I might have picked up a parasite on my trip.

"Everything looks fine, Reverend Bernal," the good doctor reported with a look of concern on his face. He proceeded to ask, "Can I tell you what I think?"

"Sure," I replied.

"You, like most men of God, feel the weight of the world on your shoulders. You are a workaholic and an over-achiever. My friend, you are burning out."

As I made my way home through the maze of rush-hour traffic, I pondered the doctor's prognosis. *Bernal, do you have a messianic complex?* I asked myself. *Is that it? Maybe all I need is two weeks in the tropics and I'll be fine.*

Something inside responded, "No, there is something wrong, very wrong!"

As the days rolled along, my staff began to take notice of my condition. Often they would come into my office and catch me sound asleep—and this after a good solid eight to nine hours of deep, deep snoozing the night before. I had a hard time keeping my train of thought. My counseling sessions were a joke. I would look at members as they poured out their hearts to me, desperately seeking help, and I could not for the life of me stay focused. At times I would see their lips moving but hear no sound coming out. *God, am I going insane?* I would scream out to myself as I struggled to hide my condition from family, staff and church.

Somehow, through the grace of God, business was being taken care of in spite of me. Our church was growing and people were genuinely getting blessed. Then I started a new series entitled "Redeemed from the Curse of the Law." As is my style, I began methodically going through the concordance and extracting every reference to curses. I was amazed at how many scriptures dealt with the subject. Since word studies fascinate me, I found myself combing libraries and Christian bookstores for more information on curse placing and curse removing. What happened next may very well have saved my ministry—and perhaps my life.

It was a beautiful fall afternoon and I was in my study at home meditating on Sunday's message. I had been teaching for a few weeks on historical curses, using for the most part biblical passages, but this Sunday it was time to deal with personal curses. These include generational or family curses, as well as curses placed on people without their knowledge. Like a bolt of lightning and a clap of thunder that resounded throughout my insides, I knew why I was sick. "My God, I've been cursed!" I shouted as I jumped to my feet.

The Curse of the Whirling Wailer

In a flash my mind went back some seven months to India. At the invitation of the Lutheran Church in Guntur, several of us young lions from America held a miracle and healing crusade for eight days. I had the opportunity to preach in four different cities. Being young in the ministry, and for that matter young in the Lord, I was full of zeal but not tempered with wisdom and experience.

I started my first service by challenging all the demons to a contest to see who was really God of all. Someone forgot to tell me that the Hindus worship over three hundred million spirits. Needless to say, we had quite a meeting. Spirits began to manifest themselves all over the place, but the Lord prevailed—except for one incident.

I will never forget her face. She was young, perhaps in her twenties. She was quite attractive, yet her eyes gave her away. Dressed like a Gypsy with plenty of jewelry and makeup, she sat right in front and seemed to be soaking up the Word. As I began to explain to the crowd the plan of salvation and how our God not only can save but also can heal and deliver, all hell broke loose. Before we could react she jumped to her feet and began to twirl and scream. Her motions and voice were inhuman. Everyone froze, including those coming forward to receive Christ. Finally, the ushers grabbed her and dragged her off into the darkness, still wailing at a pitch that sent a chill down my spine.

It took me a few minutes to recover. Many people did come forward for salvation, but others left in fear. The next evening the team sent me to another town some forty miles away. No one announced who would be speaking at what locations until it was time to depart.

The crowd here was much larger than the night before, and I felt quite ready for whatever might arise. Again, I challenged the local spirits to come and behold the power of God. I felt like an anointed Wyatt Earp at the O.K. Corral.

Everything went extremely well, or so I thought. The message was plain and simple, and I could sense that a great harvest was about to be brought in. As I invited one and all to come to Jesus, I caught her out of the corner of my eye. Twirling and screeching, she flew across the front of the crowd like a dervish from hell. Again, all stood stunned by this intruder. Finally, those in charge of maintaining order seized her and carried her off.

How did she know I would be here tonight? I asked myself. *Who is she?* We again had a good altar call but I couldn't help wondering what could have happened if she hadn't shown up and scared the people.

The next night the team sent me way out into the boonies. I was ready for her this time, I thought. Sure enough, the same exact scenario as on the two nights before began to play out. Instead of waiting for the ushers, I jumped off the crude platform, grabbed the woman and carried her a good two hundred yards out into a vacant field. I began to confront the spirits in her, but they fought me like pit bulls. They laughed at me, mocked Jesus, spit, bit, hissed and rolled the woman's eyes. They did everything but come out.

Confused, tired and angry, I stood over her as she lay on the ground. We just stared at each other for the longest time. Then she sat up with a smile and began to make symbols in the dirt, touching my feet with the dirt and chanting. I did nothing but watch out of curiosity; I have no idea why, but I did. I never saw her again.

That night in my run-down hotel room I fell deathly ill. I became semi-delirious with fever and I shook uncontrollably. *Must be something I ate or drank,* I told myself. A few days later, we all headed back to the states.

Now, seven months later, I stood in my office reliving the whole thing again and again. I began to pray to God, "Heavenly Father, your servant has been cursed. In the name of Jesus, free me from that woman's hold. This curse is causeless and I send it back from where it came."

Within forty-eight hours my strength and stamina of both body and mind returned, and I am well today. My experience would help many in the years to come.

The Effects of Ignorance and Fear

A few years after the encounter in India, I received a phone call from Linda Martinez. Linda is the wife of Charlie Martinez, a friend for over twenty years. Charlie, an evangelist, holds a black belt in Korean Karate.

"Pastor, Charlie is in the hospital and I'm afraid he is going to die," cried Linda.

"What's wrong with him?" I asked.

"They don't know, pastor. They can't find anything wrong, but he is fading fast." We came into a prayer of agreement, quoting the Word over Charlie and binding the spirit of infirmity, in the name of Jesus. Charlie pulled through, but he was a shell of his former self. A few weeks later Charlie made an appointment to come in and see me. I watched as he labored to climb the few steps to my office. Here this big, strong man was struggling to breathe. His eyes were sad and his countenance dark.

I had a feeling I knew what was wrong but I needed more information to be sure. "Charlie," I asked, "What have you been doing in ministry for the past twelve months?" He began to tell me about his work among some Indian tribes, and how the shaman had been furious with Charlie for bringing the gospel.

"Charlie, you've been cursed by their witch doctor," I declared. I proceeded to share my story to comfort my brother. Immediately we found the right scriptures and did warfare in the Spirit.

Today, Charlie Martinez is alive and well—and a little wiser. My friend Charlie and I are not isolated, unique cases. Curses are real! For us, ignorance was our enemy. "The truth shall make you free" (John 8:32). Our lack of knowledge nearly destroyed us, but God was merciful. In other cases, fear and superstition can act as magnets for curse placing. Job said,

"For the thing I greatly feared has come upon me, and what I dreaded has happened to me."

Job 3:25

Several years ago I met an evangelist from Tulsa, Oklahoma, who worked among Indians. Joe was a likable sort, big and handsome with a cheerful spirit. Joe dropped dead in the pulpit one evening as he was leading the song service.

A friend of mine told me why he believed that Joe had left this planet too early. My friends Larry and Joe had held some revival services together on reservations around the Tulsa area. Joe had been afraid of the medicine man and had voiced his concerns to Larry more than once. One night after a tent meeting Larry's new car had all but fallen apart as they were leaving the reservation. Larry had laughed it off. He had known that the medicine man had cursed his car, but had felt little concern. Joe, however, had turned pale with fear. Not long after this, his heart had just stopped.

This book is being written to educate all of us on how to break, lift, cancel and send back curses. We will also look at how and why God places curses, and how believers can learn to curse the fruitless fig trees in their lives.

And Peter, remembering, said to Him, "Rabbi, look! The fig tree which You cursed has withered away."

Mark 11:21

Chapter 2

Rebellion: The Root Cause

In this book we'll be looking at cursed races, nations, cities, families and individuals. The average American Christian has little understanding of the power of curses, yet most believers on the mission field are well aware of their evil potential.

Before moving on, let's define exactly what a curse is.

Curse n.

1. A prayer for harm to befall someone or something.
2. The harm resulting from an invocation.
3. A profane oath.
4. Something bringing or causing harm; scourge.

Curse v.

To call evil down on, to swear.

(Websters II—*New Riverside Desk Dictionary*)

In the Old Testament the Hebrew word most commonly used for this concept, translated "curse" in English, is the word "arar." Simply defined, the root word means "to execrate, to abhor or detest someone or something." This word is found in Deuteronomy chapters 27 and 28, the passages that deal with blessings and cursings. "Cursed be he that..."

Several other Hebrew words were used to describe curses and cursing. These carry such meanings as "to bind under with an oath, to pierce, to vilify, to stab with words or to blaspheme."

In the New Testament the Greek words and their meanings are very similar to those in the Old Testament. Essentially, a curse removes the blessing of God and all that goes with it. Life itself is an expression of choice between being blessed or being cursed. The 28th chapter of Deuteronomy speaks of the blessings of obedience to God's laws and the curses of rebellion against them. Then we read in chapter 30, verse 19: "I call heaven and earth as witnesses today against you, that I have set before you life and death, blessing and cursing; therefore choose life, that both you and your descendants may live." The key to the whole thing seems to revolve around two words: *obedience* and *rebellion*!

Scene 1: Adam and Eve

The clearest example of this dichotomy is found in the creation story. God had blessed man and woman.

So God created man in His own image; in the image of God He created him; male and female He created them. Then God blessed them, and God said to them,

"Be fruitful and multiply; fill the earth and subdue it; have dominion over the fish of the sea, over the birds of the air, and over every living thing that moves on the earth."

Genesis 1:27-28

Along with the blessing came responsibility.

*Then the **Lord** God took the man and put him in the garden of Eden to tend and keep it. And the **Lord** God commanded the man, saying, "Of every tree of the garden you may freely eat; but of the tree of the knowledge of good and evil you shall not eat, for in the day that you eat of it you shall surely die."*

Genesis 2:15-17

But Adam and Eve rebelled against God's command, and curses followed. It is important to note that God didn't curse Adam and Eve, whom He had blessed earlier. It was the ground God cursed because of their rebellion.

Then to Adam He said, "Because you have heeded the voice of your wife, and have eaten from the tree of which I commanded you, saying, 'You shall not eat of it': Cursed is the ground for your sake; in toil you shall eat of it all the days of your life. Both thorns and thistles it shall bring forth for you, and you shall eat the herb of the field. In the sweat of your face you shall eat bread till you return to the ground, for out of it you were taken; for dust you are, and to dust you shall return."

Genesis 3:17-19

Did you notice that along with God's command to Adam and Eve came a warning? "But of the tree of the knowledge of good and evil you shall not eat, for in the day that you eat of it you shall surely die" (2:17). As teachers and ministers of the gospel—the Good News—we often tend to emphasize the blessings of following Jesus but neglect to warn people about the consequences of disobedience. Satan rebelled and got kicked out of Heaven. Adam rebelled and got kicked out of the Garden. Humanity rebels and gets kicked out of the blessings.

Paul seemed to take the ministry of warning quite seriously. (See Acts 20:31, Colossians 1:28, 1 Thessalonians 5:14). That's why every year in our church I teach on both the blessings and the responsibilities of being a follower of our Lord. We're told to "count the cost," as well as count our blessings.

Scene 2: Noah, Ham and Canaan

Webster defines rebellion as "open opposition to any authority." Let's go back to Genesis for a sobering look at another form of rebellion.

And Noah began to be a farmer, and he planted a vineyard. Then he drank of the wine and was drunk, and became uncovered in his tent. And Ham, the father of Canaan, saw the nakedness of his father, and told his two brothers outside. But Shem and Japheth took a garment, laid it on both their shoulders, and went backward and covered the nakedness of their father. Their faces were turned

*away, and they did not see their father's nakedness.
So Noah awoke from his wine, and knew what his
younger son had done to him. Then he said: "Cursed
be Canaan; a servant of servants he shall be to his
brethren." And he said: "Blessed be the Lord, the
God of Shem, and may Canaan be his servant. May
God enlarge Japheth, and may he dwell in the tents
of Shem; and may Canaan be his servant."*

Genesis 9:20-27

A sad commentary to this tragic passage is that God had
first pronounced a blessing on all of them.

*So God blessed Noah and his sons, and said to them:
"Be fruitful and multiply, and fill the earth."*

Genesis 9:1

What brought the curse on Canaan—a curse that is still
operating today in one form or another? First of all, Noah
got drunk. Here is a clear act of rebellion; the Bible says
drunkenness is sin. Having a vineyard or even partaking of
the fruit of the vine in moderation was acceptable, but getting "plowed" meant Noah had gone too far. Then, while
old Noah was passed out, in walked his son Ham and, apparently, Ham's son Canaan. They saw the nakedness of
Noah and couldn't wait to blab it to Shem and Japheth.
(Some commentators submit that there might even have
been some act of perversion between Ham or Canaan and
sleeping Noah.) My point is this: Even though you may be
an eyewitness to another's weakness with cold, hard

documented facts, the trumpeting of another's sin is blatantly inviting a curse upon yourself.

Shem and Japheth covered their father's nakedness without even looking. Here is a lesson for today. If we look hard and long enough, we will find fault. So why go looking? No Christ-like believer can truly enjoy the fall of a brother or sister. On the contrary, there is a blessing in covering another's shortcomings.

Hatred stirs up strife, But love covers all sins.
Proverbs 10:12

Blessed is he whose transgression is forgiven, Whose sin is covered.
Psalm 32:1

The first atonement, or covering, was performed by God Himself. Take a look at Genesis 3:21:

*Also for Adam and his wife the **Lord** God made tunics of skin, and clothed them.*

Here we see sinful Adam and Eve being covered by a blood sacrifice, guilty humans being clothed by the skin of an innocent animal or animals. Some suggest that this animal was a ram, foreshadowing a later and greater atonement by the One who would lift the "curse of the law."

Chapter 3

The Nature and Operation of Blessings and Curses

Both blessings and curses are characterized by a particular kind of nature and operation. Just as a blessing is a gift, a curse is a debt. This is their nature, a truth Moses expected to be emphatically understood by God's people. The Lord had some careful instruction for His people before they crossed over into the Promised Land.

"Behold, I set before you today a blessing and a curse: the blessing, if you obey the commandments of the Lord your God which I command you today; and the curse, if you do not obey the commandments of the Lord your God, but turn aside from the way which I command you today, to go after other gods which you have not known. And it shall be, when the Lord your God has brought you into the land which you go to possess, that you shall put the blessing on

Mount Gerizim and the curse on Mount Ebal. Are they not on the other side of the Jordan, toward the setting sun, in the land of the Canaanites who dwell in the plain opposite Gilgal, beside the terebinth trees of Moreh? For you will cross over the Jordan and go in to possess the land which the Lord your God is giving you, and you will possess it and dwell in it. And you shall be careful to observe all the statutes and judgments which I set before you today."

Deuteronomy 11:26-32

Blessings and curses operate by predetermined laws in the same way that God has established the natural laws of creation. Most of us wouldn't dare test God's application of the law of gravity by jumping off high-rise buildings. And yet many people think that because they are somehow "special" cases, God will intervene and alter the nature and operation of blessings and curses just for them.

A young couple living together out of wedlock came to me to find out why they weren't blessed. They were praying, giving and attending church, yet not experiencing the blessing of God. When I asked them why they weren't married they just looked at each other and shrugged their shoulders. "Pastor, we have two children and we've been together for several years."

"You need to get married now," I firmly replied. These new converts simply had no awareness of the laws that govern blessings and curses. Once enlightened, they agreed to hold the ceremony.

Many couples or individuals come to me for financial counseling. Before their appointment, I pull their giving record up on the computer. Then after listening to their sad story of lack, I bring them to Malachi 3.

*"For I am the **Lord**, I do not change; therefore you are not consumed, O sons of Jacob. Yet from the days of your fathers you have gone away from My ordinances and have not kept them. Return to Me, and I will return to you," says the **Lord** of hosts. "But you said, 'In what way shall we return?' Will a man rob God? Yet you have robbed Me! But you say, 'In what way have we robbed You?' In tithes and offerings. You are cursed with a curse, for you have robbed Me, even this whole nation. Bring all the tithes into the storehouse, that there may be food in My house, and prove Me now in this," says the **Lord** of hosts, "if I will not open for you the windows of heaven and pour out for you such blessing that there will not be room enough to receive it."*

Malachi 3:6-10

These folks genuinely loved the Lord, but didn't realize their affection wasn't enough to work the blessings. Relationship with God, like any relationship, involves standards. We must recognize God's laws, acknowledge them, embrace them as truth and draw from them, because they reveal His character and will.

A Harvest of Evil

A sinner or saint who comes into conflict with these laws can and will reap the effects in spirit, soul, body and estate. The maladies of Deuteronomy chapter 28 cover all these areas.

> *"But it shall come to pass, if you do not obey the voice of the Lord your God, to observe carefully all His commandments and His statutes which I command you today, that all these curses will come upon you and overtake you: Cursed shall you be in the city, and cursed shall you be in the country. Cursed shall be your basket and your kneading bowl. Cursed shall be the fruit of your body and the produce of your land, the increase of your cattle and the offspring of your flocks. Cursed shall you be when you come in, and cursed shall you be when you go out. The Lord will send on you cursing, confusion, and rebuke in all that you set your hand to do, until you are destroyed and until you perish quickly, because of the wickedness of your doings in which you have forsaken Me."*
>
> Deuteronomy 28:15-20

> *"The Lord will strike you with consumption, with fever, with inflammation, with severe burning fever, with the sword, with scorching, and with mildew; they shall pursue you until you perish."*
>
> Deuteronomy 28:22

> *"The Lord will strike you with madness and blindness and confusion of heart. And you shall grope at noonday, as a blind man gropes in darkness; you shall not prosper in your ways; you shall be only*

oppressed and plundered continually, and no one shall save you."

Deuteronomy 28:28-29

"*Your sons and your daughters shall be given to another people, and your eyes shall look and fail with longing for them all day long; and there shall be no strength in your hand.*"

Deuteronomy 28:32

"*The **Lord** will bring you and the king whom you set over you to a nation which neither you nor your fathers have known, and there you shall serve other gods—wood and stone.*"

Deuteronomy 28:36

"*Moreover all these curses shall come upon you and pursue and overtake you, until you are destroyed, because you did not obey the voice of the **Lord** your God, to keep His commandments and His statutes which He commanded you.*"

Deuteronomy 28:45

What are some of the symptoms one might suffer under a curse? Deuteronomy 28 gives us some examples; I have listed others below. Let me add a word of caution here. Just because you or someone you know is afflicted in one or more of the ways mentioned, that doesn't prove the existence of a curse. But don't discount it, either.

Here is a partial list of common symptoms of curses.

1. Disturbed sleep
2. Nightmares

3. Headaches
4. Depression
5. Generational alcoholism
6. Unexplainable fatigue
7. A rash of accidents
8. Suicidal thoughts
9. Memory lapses
10. Confusion
11. Hampered breathing
12. Heart palpitation
13. Outbursts of anger
14. Premature death (especially running in one gender of a family)
15. Constant financial woes

Watch Out, Pastor!

Pastors, missionaries and evangelists need to be on constant guard against such afflictions. Most, especially those in high-visibility positions, are being cursed daily by witches, covens and the like. How many times have ministers found themselves embroiled in marital spats, conflicts with rebellious children, staff mutinies, financial problems—often seeming to come on almost overnight? Often these situations go beyond natural explanation.

How can we protect ourselves against such curses, and what can we do about it if we find ourselves cursed? The most important first step in breaking a curse is to repent for allowing it to come.

Like a flitting sparrow, like a flying swallow,
So a curse without cause shall not alight.

Proverbs 26:2

If you are suffering under the torment of a curse, some-how it found an opening. Do not get caught up with defend-ing yourself—just repent. Also, make sure you relinquish any bitterness or unforgiveness in your heart. Take your rightful authority over the curse in the name of Jesus and rebuke it. I also like to apply the blood of Christ along with His name when loosing someone or something from a curse.

Many people need teaching on what activities invite a curse, which in turn provides a platform for evil spirits.

" *'And the person who turns after mediums and familiar spirits, to prostitute himself with them, I will set My face against that person and cut him off from his people.' "*

Leviticus 20:6

Also he made his son pass through the fire, practiced soothsaying, used witchcraft, and consulted spiritists and mediums. He did much evil in the sight of the Lord, to provoke Him to anger.

II Kings 21:6

If you have ever been involved with fortune tellers, spiritists, palm readers, tarot cards, Ouija boards, cults, hyp-nosis, witchcraft, seances, astrology or the like, put this book down right now and repent and renounce your involvement.

Ask God for mercy, and break free from any hold these
would have on you.

Chapter 4

Generational Curses

Recently I was playing golf with a friend of mine from Minnesota. I noticed one of his hands was slightly deformed. When I inquired about it he replied, "Do you know what this is?" Before I could respond he went on to answer his own question. "It is a curse. This is very common in men of my nationality," he added.

My friend had identified an important truth. Certain diseases seem to operate prolifically through various families or even races. These are called generational curses.

I was listening to a tape series by Marilyn Hickey and she brought up a good point. "Do you know that doctors know more about curses than most preachers do?" she asked.

Think about it. What is the first thing you do when you visit a doctor's office? You fill out a form and check off any diseases or problems in your family on both your parents' sides. Marilyn was absolutely on target. Doctors want to know if you are cursed with a family curse. They may not call it that, but in essence that is what they are looking for.

"Did your dad have cancer, heart problems, high blood pressure? Was anyone on your mother's side afflicted with respiratory problems, arthritis, lupus?" You have probably filled out one of those forms and wondered, "What's the big deal here?" The "big deal" is that a recurring family problem will continue to afflict future generations unless the curse is broken.

Physical diseases are not the only ways generational curses can manifest themselves. A minister friend of mine told me that when he and his wife got married, the first thing they did was break the chains of the past. Pride, arrogance and alcoholism seemed to run in his wife's family and she didn't want to conceive a child until they had broken free from the curse.

Even when children are reared apart from their natural families, as in adoption, generational curses can follow them. In some cases, it takes more than a loving Christian environment to mold a young life. I personally know of two adoptive families who were tormented with confusion by generational curses. In one of the families, a girl raised in a good home began to take on the exact same characteristics and habits as her natural mother, whom she had never met. In the other case, a young lad would become dangerously enraged and hurt other children for no reason. His adoptive parents were sweet, gentle, praying people, yet they had a virtually uncontrollable child on their hands.

Christian couples who adopt should immediately free their new son or daughter from generational curses both known and unknown. These spirits should be named (if possible), renounced and told that their evil assignment is over, in the name of Jesus. Apply His blood to the past and boldly proclaim your future and your children's future in Christ.

Idolatry, Old and New

Let's look at a potent biblical example of generational curses.

And God spoke all these words, saying: "I am the Lord your God, who brought you out of the land of Egypt, out of the house of bondage. You shall have no other gods before me. You shall not make for yourself any carved image, or any likeness of anything that is in heaven above, or that is in the earth beneath, or that is in the water under the earth; you shall not bow down to them nor serve them. For I, the Lord your God, am a jealous God, visiting the iniquity of the fathers on the children to the third and fourth generations of those who hate Me, but showing mercy to thousands, to those who love Me and keep My commandments.

Exodus 20:1-6

The history of the Jewish people reveals that much of their grief can be traced to blatant violations of the first and second commandments against polytheism and image worship. *"For I, the Lord your God, am a jealous God..."*

Notice that the consequences of sin fall not just on the guilty perpetrators but on their children to the third and fourth generations as well.

This generational "visiting of iniquity" is directly linked to idolatry. The temptation to worship idols is graphically seen in the biblical account of Moses' stay on Mount Sinai.

Now when the people saw that Moses delayed coming down from the mountain, the people gathered together to Aaron, and said to him, "Come, make us gods that shall go before us; for as for this Moses, the man who brought us up out of the land of Egypt, we do not know what has become of him." And Aaron said to them, "Break off the golden earrings which are in the ears of your wives, your sons, and your daughters, and bring them to me." So all the people broke off the golden earrings which were in their ears, and brought them to Aaron. And he received the gold from their hand, and he fashioned it with an engraving tool, and made a molded calf. Then they said, "This is your god, O Israel, that brought you out of the land of Egypt!"

Exodus 32:1-4

Human beings like to worship things they can see and touch. God knows graven images inevitably will lead His people astray through their demonic power to deceive.

We in the Western world today may not experience any great temptation to create graven images, but in fact many are already made for us. An idol is that which has your heart. How many contemporary "images" keep us from God, church, prayer, Bible study and fellowship?

Our jobs.

Our homes.

Our hobbies.

Our families.

Our friends.

Our ministries.

It is amazing how we can justify our lack of true worship and defend our habits and patterns. As a pastor, I have heard every excuse and used a few of them myself. Apparently what we do not recognize is that our life-styles affect much more than just us. We are placing either a blessing or a curse on future family members as well.

The good news in all this is found in comparing the relative power of a "curse" with that of a "blessing."

"...you shall not bow down to them nor serve them. For I, the Lord your God, am a jealous God, visiting the iniquity of the fathers on the children to the third and fourth generations of those who hate Me, but showing mercy to thousands, to those who love Me and keep My commandments."

Exodus 20:5-6

Notice that the curse lasts to the third and fourth generations, but the blessings of obedience flow to thousands (of generations). The effects of good far outweigh those of evil.

Oh, do not remember former iniquities against us!
Let Your tender mercies come speedily to meet us,
For we have been brought very low.
Help us, O God of our salvation,
For the glory of Your name;
And deliver us, and provide atonement for our sins,
For Your name's sake!

Psalm 79:8-9

Breaking Generational Curses

The most pressing question I'm asked when I do a seminar on this topic is, "How do I break this type of curse off myself and my children?" The Bible tells us to lay the ax to the tree.

"And even now the ax is laid to the root of the trees.
Therefore every tree which does not bear good fruit
is cut down and thrown into the fire."

Matthew 3:10

In Jesus Christ we have a new family tree—the tree of Calvary, where all sin was nailed and remitted. There Jesus lifted the "curse of the law" off all of us. To break a family curse one must totally embrace the laws of God.

We all know "believers" who still seem to be cursed. How can this be? The issue is not believing, but obeying. James tells us in chapter 2, verses 19 and 20:

"You believe that there is one God. You do well. Even
the demons believe—and tremble! But do you want

to know, O foolish man, that faith without works is dead?"

The mark of blessed Christians is not so much what they know, but what they do. How badly do you want to be free? Badly enough to obey the Lord in whatever He asks? This is a very important question for all of us. Obedience is learned. We're not born with it. In fact, just the opposite is true. Our flesh is rebellious toward God. The unrenewed mind is hostile toward righteousness. Even Jesus our Lord had to learn obedience.

...though He was a Son, yet He learned obedience by the things which He suffered.

Hebrews 5:8

Uh-oh! There is the "s" word: suffer! Why does this word terrify us? Somehow suffering has gotten a bad rap. We seem to confuse godly suffering with the attacks of the devil. Sickness, disease, poverty and death are not lessons sent from God to perfect us, even though God can turn a curse into a blessing. These are devices of the enemy who comes to kill, steal and destroy.

What then is godly suffering? It means being hated, reviled, persecuted, lied about, maligned by family and friends for the sake of the gospel.

"Blessed are those who are persecuted for righteousness' sake, for theirs is the kingdom of heaven."

Matthew 5:10

Yes, and all who desire to live godly in Christ Jesus will suffer persecution.

II Timothy 3:12

For I consider that the sufferings of this present time are not worthy to be compared with the glory which shall be revealed in us.

Romans 8:18

Following Christ does not make you popular with the masses. Throughout life, you will have to make choices to either please people or please God.

Dying to Self-Will

As I was being prepared for full-time ministry, my wife Carla and I attended a healing crusade in Anaheim, California, back in the late 1970's. I was new to all this. The preacher called all those who had a heart condition to come forward for prayer. My father had died in his mid-fifties of a massive heart attack, and since my childhood I had had a fluttering heart. Carla used to lay her head on my chest to listen to my heart's irregular beat. When the man of God called out to those with heart problems, she almost pushed me to the front.

As he prayed for me, I felt a tangible presence blow through my being like a fresh sea breeze. It startled me so much that I looked around to see if the air conditioner had just come on. When I returned to my seat, I shared my experience with Carla. That night my wife listened intently to my heart. For the first time in years it beat normally. To this day it is still strong.

What broke me free from the Bernal curse? I believe with all my heart that it was my willingness to do the will of my Heavenly Father, to obey the call to come. Again, we read in Galatians 3:13-14:

Christ has redeemed us from the curse of the law, having become a curse for us (for it is written, "Cursed is everyone who hangs on the tree"), that the blessings of Abraham might come upon the Gentiles in Christ Jesus, that we might receive the promise of the Spirit through faith.

Before the blessings of Abraham could come upon us Gentiles, the curse had to be broken off us. Jesus lifted the curse by dying for us, by hanging on the cross (tree). The precedent for this particular type of capital punishment is found in Deuteronomy 21:22-23:

"If a man has committed a sin worthy of death, and he is put to death, and you hang him on a tree, his body shall not remain overnight on the tree, but you shall surely bury him that day, so that you do not defile the land which the Lord your God is giving you as an inheritance; for he who is hanged is accursed of God."

Here we read about a man worthy of death because of sin. He is to be hung on a tree, buried before sundown so the land is not defiled. This is exactly what happened to our Lord.

For He made Him who knew no sin to be sin for us,
that we might become the righteousness of God in
Him.

II Corinthians 5:21

"Worthy is the Lamb who was slain..."

Revelation 5:12

Jesus broke the curse by laying down His life for others.
We too have our cross to bear—dying to self that we may
live for others.

"And he who does not take his cross and follow after
Me is not worthy of Me. He who finds his life will lose
it, and he who loses his life for My sake will find it."

Matthew 10:38-39

A minister's wife made an appointment with me. When
she came in I noticed that her face was puffy from crying.
As she sat down, she told me her marriage was in great
jeopardy because of a family curse. She explained that she
had been raised by a very strong mother and grandmother.
The men in her family were weak and gave in to this
matriarchal clan.

"We drive the men in our family either crazy or away,"
she cried. "Please, Pastor Dick, break this curse off me,"
she pleaded. "I love my husband. I want to be a submissive
wife but this thing keeps coming on me."

I shared with her that freedom would take more than just
my prayers. It would require an all-out effort on her part to
die to self-will. Her spirit was willing but her flesh was
weak. Soon afterwards she and her husband were divorced.

Chapter 5

Entrances for Evil

"As he loved cursing, so let it come to him;
As he did not delight in blessing, so let it be far from
him.
As he clothed himself with cursing as with his garment,
So let it enter his body like water,
And like oil into his bones.
Let it be to him like the garment which covers him,
And for a belt with which he girds himself continually.
Let this be the Lord's reward to my accusers,
And to those who speak evil against my person."

Psalm 109:17-20

Pagans, witches and those who work the "craft" often hesitate to curse a believer. They know quite well that the curse, like a programmed missile, will find a target, and if the Christian resists in faith, the curse will come back to them. To ensure that this doesn't happen they tend to target those weak in the faith—the "believer" who isn't an "obeyer," the "hearer" who balks at being a "doer." Among the easiest victims are those who discredit the power of the Holy Spirit and rely on mental assent for their protective armor. This kind will, more than likely, deny the very existence of curses, spells, hexes and the like. The powers of darkness thrive on ignorance.

> *"My people are destroyed for lack of knowledge. Because you have rejected knowledge..."*
>
> Hosea 4:6

Ignorance is not the only point of vulnerability. What was it Satan found in Peter and the other disciples that allowed him to get permission to sift them like wheat?

> *And the Lord said, "Simon, Simon! Indeed, Satan has asked for you [all], that he may sift you as wheat. But I have prayed for you, that your faith should not fail; and when you have returned to Me, strengthen your brethren."*
>
> Luke 22:31-32

It very well could have been pride, as we look back to verses 23 and 24:

> *Then they began to question among themselves, which of them it was who would do this thing. But there was also rivalry among them, as to which of them should be considered the greatest.*

Jesus constantly reminds all of His followers:

> *"Therefore take heed that the light which is in you is not darkness."*
>
> Luke 11:35

Trauma—Gateway to Evil

How does a curse or stronghold get its initial power? One source is trauma. Nations, cities, families and individuals have been traumatized by wars, famines, earthquakes, fires, accidents and abuse of all kinds, to name a few things. The far-reaching emotional effects of such traumas can bind their victims like the tentacles of an octopus.

One evening in Seoul, Korea, Carla and I got into a deep conversation with Dr. Peter Wagner and his wife Doris about this very subject. The Wagners shared some insights they have gleaned from Cindy Jacobs, one of America's top prayer warriors and personal intercessor for Peter and Doris. Cindy is convinced that trauma is truly a gateway for evil. Trauma brings confusion, rejection, fear and other spirits that quickly take advantage of the situation. For instance, at the end of World War II, General Douglas MacArthur begged America to send 10,000 missionaries to Japan while its people were crushed in spirit and willing to listen, but we failed to do so. Instead, the forces of evil exploited their vulnerability, and now post-war Japan is one of the toughest mission fields on planet Earth. We didn't strike while the iron was hot, but Satan did.

In my ministry, I have seen many other examples of the demonic potential of trauma. Two evil spirits will immediately enter a child who has been molested. Their names are rejection and rebellion. If these children are not delivered in Jesus' name, they will grow up emotionally warped. I have yet to deal with a homosexual seeking freedom who hasn't been abused in one way or another. Our prisons are full of the rebellious and the rejected.

On New Year's day of 1990, the first day of this uniquely important decade closing out the millennium, Carla and I along with seventy other believers were in Tiananmen Square in Beijing, China. Six months earlier the now infamous massacre had taken place. We have learned that violence and murder serve as magnets for demon strongholds, and so this day we were on a mission from God. With anointing oil (Isaiah 10:27), worship, prayers and decrees, we broke the stronghold in the Spirit over Tiananmen Square. While armed guards looked on nearby, we blessed China and cursed communism. Within a few days, martial law was lifted and the citizens of Beijing were allowed back on the square.

A few months later, Ron Kenoly and I were holding a seminar in Harlingen, Texas, at the invitation of Pastor Ron Corzine. (I love preaching in Texas. The ruling princes of pride, violence and greed are probably sick of my continually coming.) Many readers will remember the horrible account of the ritual killings in Matamoros, Mexico, in the spring of 1989. Humans, including a young Texas college student, were sacrificed to Satan to protect a drug ring from getting busted. They believed Satan would protect them through blood sacrifices. Matamoros is only a few miles from Harlingen, so I asked Pastor Corzine if we could visit the site of the killings. Ron's church is a warring church so he eagerly agreed to go down to the "Ranch of Death."

Five of us, with our anointing oil and the prayers of Ron's church, headed for the Rio Grande. For days the weather had been very gloomy. Large, dark, ominous clouds hung low over the Rio Grande Valley. The air was thick.

As we crossed the border into Mexico, I felt ill. My first thought was that I had had too much coffee and that the acid was burning my stomach. But this was different. Fear began to work upon me as we approached the ranch. It was a strange sensation. I began to pray quietly for peace and strength.

The ranch had been guarded heavily by the local authorities, especially now at the one-year anniversary of the killings, so we didn't know how close to the property we would be able to get. To our surprise and joy, no one was around. Very slowly, we drove onto the ranch. There wasn't much talking as we stared at the bleak remains of an ordinary-looking Mexican ranch. One by one, we piled out of our vehicle.

As we stood on the land, Ron Kenoly led us in a song of praise and worship. We then went into warfare. Pouring the oil on the ground we broke the powers of darkness and fear off the area in our Lord's name. We reminded the territorial ruler that our Master had defeated its master and made a show of him openly.

Having disarmed principalities and powers, He made a public spectacle of them, triumphing over them in it.

Colossians 2:15

This went on for thirty minutes or so. When we all felt we had accomplished what we set out to do, we closed with a hearty "Hallelujah and amen!" That very second, the heavens parted and the sun broke through, flooding the ranch with light. We all looked at each other with one of those "could-it-be?" looks. Was God Almighty giving us a sign in the heavenlies that a breakthrough had taken place? Let me tell you, there were five believers headed back to Texas who sure thought so!

Soul Bonding

One way a curse can take hold is when a marriage, friendship or some partnership goes sour. Love, loyalty and commitment are good, but if these wonderful qualities become more fixed on human beings than on God, there can be dire results.

The term "soul bonding" can be understood by such words as "ties," "cleaving," or "knitting." Let me emphasize that there is a positive side to this.

Therefore a man shall leave his father and mother and be joined to his wife, and they shall become one flesh.

Genesis 2:24

One of my favorite stories in the Old Testament, found in 1 Samuel 18:1, illustrates a positive soul bonding:

And it was so, when he had finished speaking to Saul, that the soul of Jonathan was knit to the soul of David, and Jonathan loved him as his own soul.

Here we see a deep friendship forming between two young men. The Bible also shows strong relationships between Abraham and Isaac, David and his men, and Paul and Timothy. Today popular evangelists may be knit with their partners, or pastors with their flocks. Nothing is wrong with this until people begin to give more of their souls to each other than to God.

Soul bonding that starts out positive and turns negative is only one way this kind of curse can take root. The bonding of one's soul to another can also take place during acts of immorality.

> ...from the nations of whom the **Lord** had said to the children of Israel, "You shall not intermarry with them, nor they with you. For surely they will turn away your hearts after their gods."
>
> I Kings 11:2

Soul bonding can even take place between a person and an ideology. Demon-inspired writings can capture one's will and enslave it to false doctrines.

How can you tell if you are trapped in soul bonding to one degree or another?

A minister friend of mine, quite well known, had submitted himself and his ministry to another pastor. This pastor began to manipulate my friend, telling him things that weren't true, turning him from his friends and generally controlling his thoughts.

My friend loved this pastor and believed everything he said. His ministry began to suffer. Others saw the problem, but couldn't convince him since those in the grip of soul bonding can be blind to reality.

Finally, the power of prayer prevailed, and my friend woke up as out of a dream. "This man has stolen my soul!" he roared over the phone to me. "I couldn't even hear from God without his help." He then broke the unholy tie by repenting and forgiving the man and himself.

I have seen many people walking through life with part of their soul captured by another. In one case, a man I know would tremble whenever a former colleague's name was mentioned. A lot of hurt and bitterness needed to be healed before that link was finally broken. This same pattern plagues many divorce cases. Sometimes even hatred is carried into another relationship, putting it in danger of falling prey to the same problems if the old ties aren't properly severed.

Special Vulnerabilities of Women

I once heard a pastor say, "Women seem to fall prey to curses more than men." As a pastor myself, I have to agree with that statement. It could have to do with the Bible's description of women as the "weaker vessels" (1 Peter 3:7), or perhaps Satan's special hatred for women that dates back to Genesis 3:15:

> *"And I will put enmity between you and the woman, and between your seed and her Seed; He shall bruise your head, and you shall bruise His heel."*

Many women seem to be either exceptionally strong in the Lord or rather weak and vulnerable. Satan got to Adam through Eve. Many men today are snared by satan through women. The problem usually stems from the man's unwillingness to lead, so the woman, out of frustration, will step into the high-priestly role.

I had a couple in my office who were in conflict because of rumors filtering through the church. Whenever I addressed the husband, the wife kept butting in and answering. She was obviously angry and convinced the rumors were true. I tried my best to talk calmly and lovingly to her husband, but he just sat there. Finally I couldn't take it anymore and said, "Dear, please be quiet. I want to hear from your husband." She ignored my request and the conversation was over.

This, my friends, is not an isolated problem. A wife seeking to break a curse off herself or her family had better come under her husband's covering and protection.

But I want you to know that the head of every man is Christ, the head of woman is man, and the head of Christ is God.

I Corinthians 11:3

Spiritually dysfunctional families are open targets for curses. Mothers playing the role of the father have unfortunately produced a generation of weak, confused, neurotic and, in some cases, homosexual men. It is worth noting the final words of the Old Testament:

"And he will turn the hearts of the fathers to the children, and the hearts of the children to their

fathers, lest I come and strike the earth with a curse."

Malachi 4:6

The God-given role of woman, wife and mother is one of great honor and reward. The misguided women's rights movement is probably doing more to curse their own than anything else.

Chapter 6

Curse Breaking and the Power of Intercession

Not long ago I was ministering on the island of Maui, which the locals refer to as "the island of the gods." My host was Dr. Jim Marocco. Dr. Marocco has spent years breaking the powers of darkness over Maui, and the fruit of his labors can be seen in his ministry. His church, a strong, growing fellowship in a land known for spewing out preachers, includes many locals who have to deal with the effects of generational bondages.

One day he was invited to a family's home to pray for a baby girl who was dying of a mysterious disorder. This family had been plagued with premature death among the females; even female animals died. As Dr. Marocco came into the room where the dying infant lay, he felt a cold presence. His attention was drawn towards an old woman sitting in the corner. The grandmother looked like death incarnate. Right away, this astute minister knew that this affliction was the work of a curse. He prayed a curse-breaking prayer, which is different than a general healing prayer or a classic deliverance prayer in that it specifically addresses the stronghold.

That evening the father of the child called Dr. Marocco to his home. As the two sat down to visit, the father blurted out, "Could this be the work of a curse?" Jim had not shared his insights with any of the family members. Now the man of God and the father were both onto the root of the problem. The little girl lived, and the women of this family would fear no more. The curse had lost its power.

Some of the stories I've heard don't always have a happy ending. A young couple fresh out of Bible school were ministering in and around the Caribbean, an area well-known for the practice of voodoo, witchcraft and curses. They were heavily involved in spiritual warfare. One afternoon as the husband was riding his motor bike down a country road, a horse that had been lazily grazing in a field suddenly jerked and headed for the fence. The crazed animal jumped the crude fence and landed squarely on the young minister, killing him instantly. A freak accident? Chance? Or could it have been a well-placed curse on a young man left unprotected through lack of intercession? I'm not sure, but it does make one stop and think.

Another bizarre incident, somewhat similar, took place in the state of Washington a couple of years back. A pastor, like many today, was researching the history of his city and area. What was he looking for? Anything that would give demonic powers a footing or a stronghold, such as broken covenants, violence, Masonic influence and the like. The pastor shared with his wife his excitement at a recent discovery he believed would blow a hole in the heavenlies. He truly felt he had located the "strongman."

The next day he and another brother went canoeing on a local river. They paddled into sacred Indian waters. The pastor's canoe flipped, and this man—though an excellent swimmer and a former lifeguard—drowned. His wife contacted me soon after the tragedy. "Pastor Dick, where did he miss it?"

"I don't know," I sadly replied. "I just don't know."

Since these and other tragedies have come to my attention, I have become increasingly aware of the need for constant intercession on behalf of spiritual warriors. Anyone who attempts to pull down a ruling prince had better be protected day and night. There are, of course, other key factors needed, such as holiness, unity in the home and the church, a heart free from bitterness, strife, envy or unforgiveness. But I am convinced that massive intercession is a must.

One of the more interesting meetings I've held recently took place in the city of Bend, Oregon. Bend is absolutely gorgeous to behold but, like all of Central Oregon, it is a hotbed of New Age activity. Pastor Phil Marocco, brother of Jim in Maui, invited me for a three-day warfare seminar. The first night, as I frequently do, I asked the people in the service to bring me books and articles on the history of Bend. My friend John Dawson has taught me that the origins of a city can usually point to the nature of the stronghold there.

The next day the local Vineyard pastor and his lovely wife invited me over for coffee and fellowship. I could feel a tenseness in the atmosphere. *Perhaps they're going through some difficulty—that's not unusual in the ministry,* I thought. The pastor's wife stared at me for a moment before asking, "Why are you here?" The tone of her voice startled me momentarily.

"Well, I am not sure why the Lord has me here, but I pray I can be a blessing and help to all of you," I responded, adding, "But, I can't promise you anything."

At this she burst into tears. *Dear God in Heaven, what did I say?* I wondered. After a few moments she recovered her composure. "I'm sorry, Pastor Dick, but thank you for being the first honest speaker we've had in a long, long time." She went on to tell me a shocking story that both angered and frustrated me. Well-known evangelists had come to town and promised the moon, raised large amounts of money for future crusades and then never returned—not even made a phone call or sent a letter. The believers of Bend were worn out by promise-breaking preachers.

That night before the service, a sister asked if she could have a word with me. "Pastor Dick, I thought this might be of some interest to you. The local Indians used to call this place 'the land of broken promises.' " Apparently the curse was still operating, and even affecting good ministers who fell under its power.

That night Ron Kenoly, my music minister, and I stood and prayed for every evangelist and pastor who had broken his word to these precious people, and begged forgiveness on their behalf. After much weeping and travailing, joy broke through.

Chapter 7

Territorial Curses

The Bible and experiential reality both seem to suggest that corporate curses can be leveled against the inhabitants of particular territories. In this chapter we'll take a look at examples of curses directed at nations and cities.

Nations Cursed

*Now the **Lord** had said to Abram: "Get out of your country, from your kindred and from your father's house, to a land that I will show you. I will make you a great nation; I will bless you and make your name great; and you shall be a blessing. I will bless those who bless you, and I will curse him who curses you; and in you all the families of the earth shall be blessed."*

Genesis 12:1-3

I wonder how many nations and even empires have come to wish they had taken this passage seriously. "I will curse him [nations] who curses you [Israel]..." (verse 3).

In Lester Sumrall's book *Jerusalem: Where Empires Die*, he pointed out how world powers have crumbled after tampering with the Holy Land and its capital city, Jerusalem. As far back as the Assyrian, Babylonian, Persian, Grecian and Roman Empires, and up to this century, would-be conquerors have ruled over that land. From 1517 to 1917, the Turks (the Ottoman Empire) controlled Palestine.

Shortly after World War I, the British and other Allied troops seized Jerusalem without firing a shot. At that time England was a strong world power. (The old saying still echoes in men's clubs throughout London today: "Remember, chaps, when the sun never set on the British Empire.") But because of her mistreatment of Israel, England, like the empires before her, began to unwind. Around the late 1930's the country started declining from good to fair to worse and things haven't reversed yet.

I pray America will continue to bless Israel and not reject her. I know the picture gets a little confusing because Israel doesn't always act like a righteous nation and the liberal humanists would love to turn on her. But let us remember Psalm 129:

"Many a time they have afflicted me from my youth,"
Let Israel now say—
"Many a time they have afflicted me from my youth;
Yet they have not prevailed against me.
The plowers plowed on my back;
They made their furrows long."
The Lord is righteous;

He has cut in pieces the cords of the wicked.
Let all those who hate Zion
Be put to shame and turned back.
Let them be as the grass on the housetops,
Which withers before it grows up,
With which the reaper does not fill his hand,
Nor he who binds sheaves, his arms.
Neither let those who pass by them say,
"The blessing of the Lord be upon you;
We bless you in the name of the Lord."

Mistreatment of Israel is only one of various reasons nations today suffer under curses. Argentina's woes can be traced to a curse put on her by Juan and Isabel Peron's secretary of social welfare, a known warlock, back in the 1970's. Since then, the nation has hit rock bottom morally, fiscally and politically. Thank God for people like Ed Silvoso, C. Peter Wagner and his wife Doris, and a host of Argentine pastors and prayer warriors who are breaking the curse off a beautiful land.

One of the most interesting meetings we have had at our church took place when Loren Cunningham came and ministered on this subject. Loren, the founder of Youth With A Mission, brought some fascinating charts comparing the quality of life in certain nations, touching on a wide spectrum of variables, ranging from income, health and longevity to ability to feed the people, the literacy rate, personal freedom and other areas. The charts came from a book he recommended, *Target Earth.*[1] This world missions overview contains invaluable information for anyone who wants to see in living color the blessing of following Christ and the consequences of following a different path.

Using data from 131 nations and colored charts, Mr. Cunningham compared the quality of life in the Christian nations with that in Islamic, Buddhist, Hindu, tribal-religious and non-religious countries—even in the Jewish nation of Israel. The difference is staggering. From this perspective alone it is clear we are following the right God and living by the right book.

It blows my mind (as my kids say) to think the New Agers of America want to pull us into a religion based primarily on Hinduism and other Eastern mystical ideas. All it should take to quash this notion is to visit India, as I have, with spiritual eyes open. Here is the proof of the pudding. Take a good look at a cursed nation. This is the fruit of demon worship.

A recent national news magazine had a picture of a tombstone on its cover with the classic hammer and sickle. The engraving read, "Death of a nation, 1917-?" Just the other day the world celebrated John Lennon's birthday by playing his hit song "Imagine" to an estimated one billion listeners. "Imagine" is the theme song and rallying cry of the New World Order, the Age of Aquarius. Its lyrics go something like this: "Imagine there's no heaven, It's easy if you try. No hell below us, Above us, only sky. Imagine all the people living for today. Imagine there's no countries, It isn't hard to do. Nothing to kill or die for, And no religion too…" I thought Karl Marx had sung that tune already, and look where it took his nation.

As I was reading an article in the *San Jose Mercury News* about all the hoopla over Lennon's birthday and the world paying him homage, I turned the page and came face to face with a picture of several poor Russian women, standing in the cold waiting hours to buy rotten apples. Yes, John, Russia imagined just what you sang about and is now cursed because of it. Yet, thank God for the believers in Russia and the intercessors outside her boundaries who have prayed and continue to pray for change. It is obvious there are some believers in formerly communist countries who know something about spiritual warfare and curse breaking. We may need to import them to America if we don't jump on our own present challenges quickly.

A book I highly recommend is *Wrestling With Dark Angels.*[2] This strategic piece of work is a collection of articles written by scholars and missionaries on the subject of strongholds, curses and bondages that must be broken through a power encounter. Pennoyer wrote "Demonization is a personal relationship, the imposition of an evil spirit into the life of a human being. The Bible contains numerous accounts of demonization, and personal case histories on the subject can be found in bookstores around the world. Much less attention has focused on the collective impact of demonized individuals in their society or subculture. We may be somewhat familiar with the classic manifestation of extreme individual demonization, such as unusual strength, other voices and disclosure of private information. But what are some of the features of a society or subculture where the majority of individuals are demonized?"[3]

A curse can cause a whole society to come under demonic influence to one degree or another. If this society happens to practice idol worship, this magnifies the problem.

In the group of primitives Pennoyer worked with, he found some interesting key features of collective captivity. First was heavy demonization at the leadership level. These leaders were more than likely controlled by the strong, high-ranking territorial spirits of that region. The second thing he found he called demonic bonding. Quoting Pennoyer: "...many individuals in the society or subculture are not only demonized but they have bonded with their demons. This bond of friendship may be especially strong with generational or kin spirits who are passed along family lines. The demon can reinforce this bond by acting as a family historian and reciting real or fabricated facts concerning the individual's ancestors."[4]

Although Pennoyer's writings are based on his experiences with the Tawbuid people in the highlands of Mindoro, Central Philippines, don't for a minute think group demonization can't happen in "civilized society." Satan's bag of tricks is the same for all classes.

Ed Silvoso has identified what he called "the 5 D's of warfare," taken from a study of Exodus 1 and 2.

First "D"—DECEPTION

Satan is the great deceiver. Notice what Pharaoh (a type of Satan) said in Exodus 1:10:

...come, let us deal wisely with them, lest they multiply, and it happen, in the event of war, that they also join our enemies and fight against us, and so go up out of the land."

Pharaoh—and Satan—purpose to deal wisely and craftily to keep people in bondage.

Second "D"—DOMINATION

Let's look at Exodus 1:11:

Therefore they set taskmasters over them to afflict them with their burdens. And they built for Pharaoh supply cities, Pithom and Raamses.

Control them, Pharaoh said, and make them build our cities for us!

Third "D"—DESTRUCTION

Look at Exodus 1:16:

...and he said, "When you do the duties of a midwife for the Hebrew women, and see them on the birthstools, if it is a son, then you shall kill him; but if it is a daughter, then she shall live."

Satan's ultimate goal was to destroy them.

Fourth and Fifth "D's"—DIVINE DELIVERANCE

Now look at Exodus 2, verses 24-25:

So God heard their groaning, and God remembered His covenant with Abraham, with Isaac, and with Jacob. And God looked upon the children of Israel, and God acknowledged them.

God help us to convince nations that are being deceived, dominated and destroyed that they must call upon the name of the Lord for divine deliverance. If they do not respond, they will have to reckon with God's warning in Leviticus 18:24-25:

> *"'Do not defile yourselves with any of these things; for by all these the nations are defiled, which I am casting out before you. For the land is defiled; therefore I visit the punishment of its iniquity upon it, and the land vomits out its inhabitants.'"*

How many times have our hearts broken while watching starving and afflicted people dying from famine and disease on some television newscast or Christian special? We send offerings to ease our conscience, but these sufferers need much more than rice, milk or a new tractor. They need the curse broken off their nation immediately.

Cities Cursed

The Bible is full of stories of cities that were cursed. Some were destroyed and never rebuilt; others repented and enjoyed a season of grace. Today, many modern cities are laboring under a curse, most of them unawares.

On my way to work the other day I was listening to a radio news talk program. The subject was, "What ever happened to beautiful San Francisco, one of America's showpieces, a world-class city, the Paris of the West?"

A caller, a dignified-sounding gentleman with a bit of a British accent, talked about the "good old days" of the city by the Bay, the fifties and sixties when San Francisco was dotted with quaint little shops and restaurants. He remembered a time when people could take evening strolls without a panhandler or hooker bumping into them, a time when you didn't see a homeless person sleeping in every other doorway or taking up every park bench, a time when it was rare to see two men kissing and openly fondling each other's private parts unashamedly in front of decent men, women and children. The city that once had a surplus of funds is now hopelessly in debt. Liberals and homosexuals dictate many of the city's laws and policies. "No wonder tourism is down over fifty percent," the caller chimed in. *All this plus killer earthquakes,* I thought to myself. Yes, and don't forget the AIDS epidemic; no one really knows when the time bomb of this horrible disease will blow up in society's face.

What has happened to beautiful San Francisco? The talk show callers tried to put a finger on it. But I had an idea they didn't mention. It's been cursed! Yet, for all this, I've seen worse. All one has to do is tour Calcutta, New Delhi, Bombay or, for that matter, any city that has rejected Jesus Christ as Lord and worships demons or self.

We all know about Sodom and Gomorrah and how the stench of their sin got God's attention. Another major city, Nineveh, nearly suffered the same fate but heeded the words of Jonah the prophet. Moreover, large portions of the books of Isaiah and Jeremiah focus on God's warnings to Jerusalem and other cities of Judah that a curse would destroy them if they didn't turn back to the Lord.

"Your country is desolate, your cities are burned with fire; strangers devour your land in your presence; and it is desolate, as overthrown by strangers."

Isaiah 1:7

Like many of you, I've traveled to the Holy Land several times to see, feel and take in that wonderfully unique little strip of earth so destined by God. As much as I love Jerusalem and have many friends there, I have a real passion for Galilee. As we read the Gospels we see a good deal of our Lord's ministry taking place in and around this region. One of the more significant stops was a city called Capernaum. Unlike most other cities that were destroyed more than once, over the last two thousand years Capernaum was never rebuilt. Why? It sits in a very beautiful place. Perhaps the answer lies in this passage:

Then He began to upbraid the cities in which most of His mighty works had been done, because they did not repent: "Woe to you, Chorazin! Woe to you, Bethsaida! For if the mighty works which were done in you had been done in Tyre and Sidon, they would have repented long ago in sackcloth and ashes. But I say to you, it will be more tolerable for Tyre and Sidon in the day of judgment than for you. And you, Capernaum, who are exalted to heaven, will be brought down to Hades; for if the mighty works which were done in you had been done in Sodom, it would have remained until this day. But I say to you

*that it shall be more tolerable for the land of Sodom
in the day of judgment than for you."*
                                    Matthew 11:20-24

Many cities will not be won to the Lord unless the curses over them are discerned and broken. Jeremiah received
a strong word from the Lord about removing a curse before
blessings could come.

> *Then the **Lord** put forth His hand and touched my
> mouth, and the **Lord** said to me: "Behold, I have put
> My words in your mouth. See, I have this day set you
> over the nations and over the kingdoms, to root out
> and to pull down, to destroy and to throw down, to
> build and to plant."*
>   Jeremiah 1:9-10

In Joshua we see a biblical model for spiritual warfare.
He conquered the Promised Land by taking one city at a
time. For more details, let me suggest that you read my
book *Come Down Dark Prince* and/or John Dawson's book
Taking Our Cities For God. Both deal in depth with this
subject.

Every year at our church we have a spiritual warfare
conference. On the last night we conclude by taking
thousands of believers to various places around San Jose
and the South Bay Area to pray and break any curse holding back God's blessings. We visit areas we know to be
strongholds, areas of influence and power. The results have
been amazing. I have encouraged many pastor friends to do

the same, and several major cities now have "breakthrough" nights.

God loves cities. The Bible is full of stories about cities. In fact, the greatest of all cities is being handcrafted right now by the Lord Himself, and will come down from heaven like a bride adorned for her husband.

Redeeming the Land

One of the great pleasures in life is meeting wonderful servants of the Lord. I am blessed to call many of them my friends. One who has much experience dealing with cursed land is Gwen Shaw. Sister Shaw heads up a ministry called End-Time Handmaidens, located in Jasper, Arkansas. A must for your library is her book *Redeeming the Land.*[5] Gwen said that in order to break a curse off a land, be it a nation, a city or just a piece of property, there are certain steps that should be followed:

1. Share your burden with others. Get only courageous and strong intercessors who live a holy life and have faith to work with you. Unholy lives can be attacked by evil spirits. You will be coming up against strong demon princes who have ruled over their areas for centuries, and your protection is your holy life, your faith and the blood of Jesus.

Gwen went on to list several key points:

2. Prepare your hearts with prayer and fasting.

3. Ask God to show you the area He wants you to go to. Locate national shrines, places where murder or suicide or innumerable car accidents have taken place and where witchcraft has been practiced.

4. Go with a group (never alone).

5. On arrival, begin to praise the Lord. [Gwen also suggested staying open to the Holy Spirit for further revelation about strongholds.]

6. Confess these sins to the Lord on behalf of the transgressors. Bring everything into the light. Demons do not like the light.

7. Exalt the Lord with high praises. Sing in the Spirit. Declare the victory.

8. Hold the Lord's Supper.
   You prepare a table before me in the presence of my enemies. Psalm 23:5

9. Ask God to send the protecting angels to camp about you.

10. Anoint the ground with oil.

11. Prophesy life and blessing to the Land.

A good way to close this particular type of curse-breaking ceremony—whether it be over land or over people—is with spontaneous praise, joy and even laughter in the Holy Spirit. I have received many testimonies from folks all over the world who read one of my books, did what I suggested and saw it work. Droughts were broken, church splits averted, marriages saved, finances restored, children set free from drugs—you name it and the curse can be broken.

Endnotes

1. Co-published by University of the Nations and Global Mapping, International; general editor, Frank Kaleb Jansen.

2. Coedited by C. Peter Wagner and F. Douglas Pennoyer, Regal Books, 1990.

3. Ibid., p. 250.

4. Ibid., p. 259-260.

5. *Redeeming the Land* by Gwen Shaw, Engeltal Press, 1987, pp. 181-186.

Chapter 8

Christian Cursing

Like the blessing, the curse is a reality. It cleaves to the sinner, pursues him, hunts him down, ruins and slays him... By *experience*. 'Rarely,' says Horace, 'has Punishment, though lame, failed to overtake the criminal fleeing before her.'

By *mythology*. It was a conviction, true alike to conscience and the facts of life, which the Greeks sought to personify in the Erinyes, in Nemesis, and in Ate, who clung to a man or to a family in punishment for some half-forgotten crime. By *literature*, which is full of the recognition of avenging powers. The Bible confirms the substance of this varied teaching, but lifts the subject out of the region of mythology.

—Pulpit Commentary,
The Book of Deuteronomy,
MacDonald Publishing Company, pp. 436-437.

Curses figure prominently in pagan or heathen sorcery. A curse may be placed by various means, including charms, incantations, potions or mixtures of diverse ingredients (some very strange ingredients, I might add). In one city in Argentina I was told of a witch who mixed oil and dirt from a graveyard to place a curse on a particular object or person. Also, during a visit to Omar Cabrera's Bible School facilities, which were still under construction, Omar's wife, Marfa, took us to a spot where a few nights before some spiritists had come onto their property and placed a curse, using candles, ashes and other items. We broke the curse and cleansed the area in prayer, praise and proclamation.

As Christians we are appalled and offended at the very thought of placing a curse on another person to ensure that our will is done in and through them. But the truth is that far too much witchcraft flourishes in churches today. What do I mean by witchcraft? I am speaking here of the spirit of control, manipulation and domination.

In Paul's upbraiding of the Galatian church he exclaimed, "O foolish Galatians! Who has bewitched you..." (Galatians 3:1). The word "bewitched" speaks of leading astray, misleading by an evil eye, working charms, bringing evil on a person by feigned praise. Clearly, someone within the Galatian church had worked witchcraft on their minds.

Paul went on later to say:

For as many as are of the works of the law are under the curse; for it is written, "Cursed is everyone who

*does not continue in all things which are written in
the book of the law, to do them."*

Galatians 3:10

In other words, those "bewitching" the believers were
cursed and trying to make others cursed as well. Paul felt
so adamantly about the evil involved that in his opening
remarks to his beloved Galatian friends he said:

*As we have said before, so now I say again, if anyone
preaches any other gospel to you than what you have
received, let him be accursed.*

Galatians 1:9

Accursed! The Greek word is "anathema." Anyone or
anything that attempts to nullify the death of Christ or
preaches another way to the Father is to be given over to
total destruction.

The Power of Words

This kind of evil manipulation doesn't have to involve
crucial points of doctrine. Our day-to-day conversations
and even our prayers can too often be laced with words
phrased to control or manipulate others. The Bible offers
both warning and advice in this regard:

*But no man can tame the tongue. It is an unruly evil,
full of deadly poison. With it we bless our God and
Father, and with it we curse men, who have been
made in the similitude of God. Out of the same
mouth proceed blessing and cursing. My brethren,
these things ought not to be so. Does a spring send*

*forth fresh water and bitter from the same opening?
Can a fig tree, my brethren, bear olives, or a
grapevine bear figs? Thus no spring can yield both
salt water and fresh. Who is wise and understanding
among you? Let him show by good conduct that his
works are done in the meekness of wisdom. But if you
have bitter envy and self-seeking in your hearts, do
not boast and lie against the truth. This wisdom does
not descend from above, but is earthly, sensual,
demonic. For where envy and self-seeking exist, confusion and every evil thing will be there. But the wisdom that is from above is first pure, then peaceable,
gentle, willing to yield, full of mercy and good fruits,
without partiality and without hypocrisy. Now the
fruit of righteousness is sown in peace by those who
make peace.*

James 3:8-18

The power of words is a subject still in great need of
research. In many ways our lives are subject to being
shaped and molded by words spoken over us. When
children are told they will never amount to anything, that
they are no good, then they will seek a way to fulfill that
curse. On the other hand, a child who is encouraged, loved
and blessed will usually grow up to be a blessing.

Authority Empowers Curses—Leaders, Beware!

A friend of mine recently shared with me a startling
revelation. The spirit world knows that Jesus has all power
and authority.

Now in the synagogue there was a man who had a spirit of an unclean demon. And he cried out with a loud voice, saying, "Let us alone! What have we to do with You, Jesus of Nazareth? Did You come to destroy us? I know You, who You are—the Holy One of God!"

Luke 4:33-34

When He had come to the other side, to the country of the Gergesenes, there met Him two demon-possessed men, coming out of the tombs, exceedingly fierce, so that no one could pass that way. And suddenly they cried out, saying, "What have we to do with You, Jesus, You Son of God? Have You come here to torment us before the time?"

Matthew 8:28-29

Also there were seven sons of Sceva, a Jewish chief priest, who did so. And the evil spirit answered and said, "Jesus I know, and Paul I know; but who are you?"

Acts 19:14-15

The demons acknowledge Jesus as the Son of God. They tremble at His name. So there is no argument in the spirit world over the authority of Christ. This is why demons start to drool whenever a preacher of the gospel gives in to the flesh and becomes angry, jealous, hurt or threatened. If a spirit can get a follower of Jesus, especially an anointed leader with recognized authority, to curse a brother or sister through irresponsible words, the curse can be extremely powerful.

It is no surprise and no big deal when the world brings an accusation against a believer. But when a respected minister writes a book defaming other ministers, the lid blows off the pressure cooker. We begin to have church splits, arguments, more discord than we need, and plenty of confused Christians.

How many times have we heard evangelists or pastors rail against another brother simply because he preaches slightly differently? One who comes to mind used to reference a brand of chewing tobacco when he would say publicly, "Copeland-Hagin, no Copenhagen! Chew it up and spit it out." I know that Ken Copeland and Kenneth Hagin are two God-fearing people who have brought the body a word on strong faith. You may not agree with them on every point of doctrine, but the body has certainly had a great need to get back to faith.

Moreover, I notice that ministers who choose to curse in this manner instead of bless seem to suffer with financial problems, marriage challenges, rebellious children and even premature death. Yet, many fail to learn or choose to ignore these truths:

Therefore you are inexcusable, O man, whoever you are who judge, for in whatever you judge another you condemn yourself; for you who judge practice the same things. But we know that the judgment of God is according to truth against those who practice such things. And do you think this, O man, you who judge those practicing such things, and doing the same, that you will escape the judgment of God?

Romans 2:1-3

Who are you to judge another's servant? To his own master he stands or falls. Indeed, he will be made to stand, for God is able to make him stand.

Romans 14:4

In some extreme cases, I've heard of pastors cursing people who left their churches for another. A friend in Dallas called and asked for my advice on a disturbing matter. A neighbor pastor was telling all the folks who left his church to join my friend's church that they would soon suffer financial difficulty as a result of leaving. Make no mistake—that is a curse!

I'm not advocating thoughtless church-hopping. I believe in authority and submission, and I tell the new prospects at our membership breakfasts to get a written release and blessing from their current pastor, if any, before joining Jubilee Christian Center. Many denominational churches have enough sense to send letters of transfer. It is a good practice we should all embrace. Even secular businesses want references so they can see if an applicant will be a blessing or a curse.

One former pastor used to tell his members they would get cancer and die if they left his church. This is a classic example of a so-called "man of God" using dark powers to control.

> *And God said to Balaam, "You shall not go with*
> *them; you shall not curse the people, for they are*
> *blessed."*
>
> Numbers 22:12

To curse God's people whom He has blessed is to bring a curse upon yourself.

Chapter 9

Reverse the Curse

Reverse the curse! Catchy little phrase, isn't it? I wish I'd thought it up, but I'm borrowing it from my friend Larry Lea. This was the war cry for our Prayer Breakthrough in San Francisco on Halloween night of 1990. Never before in the history of a Christian event was there so much interest from the media. We were all caught off guard, to say the least.

It began innocently enough. Dr. Lea held a breakfast for Bay Area ministers to see if we all thought it a good idea to hold such a meeting on such a night in such a city. The consensus was, "Yes and amen! Let's go for it!" For Larry to unite so many churches in one of America's toughest areas of ministry was our first breakthrough.

The *San Francisco Chronicle* called to ask my opinion about the planned crusade. Don Lattin, the editor of the religion section, already knew something about me and our church, and he was aware that we went to the high places every year to pull down certain ruling princes over the Bay Area. He asked me to name some of them, so I did.

I told Don that San Francisco was held in the grip of the spirit of perversion and rejection. Oakland, I said, was ruled by violence and hopelessness. In San Jose we saw a spirit of mammon, in Santa Cruz the occult, and in Marin County the New Age. Addiction held sway in the Vallejo/Richmond area, pharmakeia or drugs in the Hayward/San Leandro area, and poverty in Watsonville. I went on to name several more strongholds of the enemy.

The next day a large article appeared in the *Chronicle* detailing the Breakthrough and my two cents of insight. The wire service picked it up, and everything broke loose. Before long our phone was ringing off the hook. The *Wall Street Journal*, *USA Today*, CNN, ABC, CBS, NBC—you name it, they wanted to know, "Who is this Larry Lea individual, what are demon powers and what in the world is a prayer warrior?"

On October 30, my forty-sixth birthday, the stories surfaced nationally. The *Wall Street Journal* put it right on the front page, calling Larry and I exorcists. (I've been called worse.) *USA Today* also ran the story, and included the name of Eric Pryor, who, the article said, claimed to be the high priest of the New Earth Temple and the head of the Bay Area Pagan Community, which he said included some 50,000 members. As a practitioner of Wicca, an ancient religion, he saw us as a threat to their beliefs and publicly issued a curse on us. The article in *USA Today* said we would fall in our pulpits, break our legs, get ill, suffer financial problems, and more.

That Tuesday, the day before Halloween—he organized 300 pagans to gather in front of the Civic Auditorium, the scene of the Breakthrough, to officially put a curse on all of us. Another group painted "Kill the Christians" all along the sidewalk. A militant faction from the homosexual community also issued threats of harm and violence if the meeting went on as planned.

By now this was front-page news in every major Bay Area newspaper, and a lead-in story on all the networks. For some reason I was seen as the local expert so my face and name were daily in front of the public, morning, afternoon and night.

After office hours on October 29, a call was placed to our church. "Hello," the somber voice on our answering machine intoned. "I am Eric Pryor." He listed his credentials before going on. This time the threat was more personal. "I hope you Christians know what you're doing. I hope you really know how to pray, because we certainly know how to curse—and we will curse." Click...end of message.

Conversation with a Pagan

On the morning of October 31, I was scheduled to be on a local CBS television talk show to discuss demons and deliverance. To my surprise, Eric Pryor was also a guest, along with a local ABC radio talk show host named Bernie Ward. Bernie has a program called "God Talk" and a rather strange philosophy, loosely based on liberal Catholicism, humanism and New Age ideology. Mr. Ward had been crucifying Larry Lea and me for weeks on his program, calling us "Jim Jones" and "snake oil" salesmen. This was going to be an interesting day.

As we were ushered into the waiting room for makeup and coffee, I remembered what my wife had shared with me the night before. When she read about Eric Pryor and the curse he had leveled at all of us and saw his picture in the newspaper, she had been filled with compassion for this lost soul. She had lain on the floor of my office clutching the article against her stomach, and had begun to travail in the Spirit. She was convinced that God was going to turn the curse into a blessing.

As Eric walked in, I could tell he was nervous. "Hello, Eric, I'm Dick Bernal. Nice to meet you," I greeted him.

"Yeah, uh-huh," came the weak reply. Bernie finally showed up and it was time to go on.

The program was a zoo, but I got my points in, as did Eric and Bernie. Afterwards I asked Eric to have coffee with Carla and me, just to talk. He quickly accepted.

Now Eric seemed much more comfortable. Perhaps it was Carla's hugs and blessings that disarmed him. Who knows? A lot was changing fast. Two hours before the Breakthrough was to begin, we sat down to talk religion, God, Jesus, the Bible, convictions, truth and a veritable plethora of subjects. In the heat of the dialogue, I said, "Eric, I really like you."

"Well, I like you too, Dick, " he responded with a big, toothy grin.

"Hey, Eric, why don't you come be my guest tonight?" I proposed. "You can sit with me and judge for yourself what a Christian is and what this meeting is really about."

"I'd like that, Dick, " he answered thoughtfully. "But first let me make a couple of phone calls. I'm calling off the demonstration from our community."

When Eric returned from his calls he had a silly look on his face. "Boy, my associates think I'm nuts going with you to hear Larry Lea preach. They can't believe it. They say it's a trap."

It began to dawn on me that some people actually believe Christians would do something like that. The burning of witches in New England a couple of centuries ago by so-called "believers" must still leave a fearful impression on modern witches.

"We're not here to burn or call fire down on anyone," I reassured him. Jesus Himself, I noted, had rebuked such a notion when His disciples got a bit self-righteous.

But they did not receive him, because His face was set for the journey to Jerusalem. And when His disciples James and John saw this, they said, "Lord, do You want us to command fire to come down from heaven and consume them, just as Elijah did?" But He turned and rebuked them, and said, "You do not know what manner of spirit you are of. For the Son

of Man did not come to destroy men's lives but to
save them." And they went to another village.

Luke 9:53-56

Breakthrough in the Spirit

We had been told to arrive early at the Civic Auditorium because of the potential for violent confrontation. As we drove up, the scene outside the auditorium looked like some crazy circus. A thousand or so homosexuals and lesbians crowded around dressed in indescribable outfits. I noticed a twelve-foot-high papier-maché penis made into a cross. There was a pink Jesus—a man spray-painted hot pink and wearing a crown of thorns. Another placard read, "God is a black lesbian." Demonstrators blocked the entrance and yelled obscenities at the Christians. Believers were spit on, kicked, scratched and cursed.

As Eric, Carla and I made our way toward the crowd, many cheered when they saw Eric. He was a sight, I must say. Eric was dressed in a priest's shirt, collar and all, with a large pentagram hanging around his neck. Strange-looking rings studded his fingers, and long, bleached blond hair flowed down his back. And there I was in my conservative, dark blue, double-breasted suit walking arm-in-arm with him through the crowd. The demonstrators just stared at this odd couple.

As we entered the huge auditorium a few mouths dropped open. Just hours before, we had been pitted one against the other on a live television talk show. Eric had publicly cursed us on national television as well as in *USA*

Today, yet here we were together. One of Larry Lea's team members came over to David Brimmer, my associate, and asked, pointing to Eric, "What is *he* doing here?"

David assured him everything was fine. "Eric has been with Pastor Dick and Carla most of the afternoon, and he's our guest here tonight."

The service was powerful, to say the least. The worship was strong, and Larry's preaching anointed. When we announced that a portion of the evening's offering would go to the homeless and other worthy causes, you could visibly see a change in our guest. Eric truly enjoyed the service.

Afterwards we spent time with the press sharing our new-found friendship. Eric went on CNN and ABC to say he had enjoyed the service and misjudged the Christians. Then he went a dangerous step further and renounced three militant fringe groups set on disrupting anything that condemns their life style: Queer Nation, GHOST (Grand Homosexual Outrage at Sickening Televangelists) and ACT-UP. By doing so, Eric had put his life in danger.

The next day the papers read, "Pagans Make Peace with Charismatics." Eric and Sandra, his girlfriend, visited again at the Breakthrough Thursday night and felt the love and power of the Holy Spirit. It seemed like Larry was preaching directly to them, but of course the Spirit of Grace ministered to everyone.

Friday morning Larry called me at my hotel room to ask if he could visit with Eric. Larry and his wife Melva were prompted to pray for Eric and felt it necessary to share with him. We arranged a meeting for 1:30 p.m. Larry's heartfelt and undeniable love for Eric shone through. Later, Carla and I had to catch a plane to Southern California to join Paul and Jan Crouch as guests on TBN that night.

The Turning Point

We stayed in contact with Eric Pryor, even while Carla and I were in Maui holding a seminar at the First Assembly of God Church. David Brimmer talked almost daily with Eric, encouraging him to stay open to the gospel. Then as soon as we returned to San Jose I called Eric to invite him to a Sunday morning service at our church.

As should be expected, opposing forces were hard at work tempting Eric to cash in on his new-found national fame. Well-known satanists, pagans and witches began calling, writing, inviting and giving suggestions to Eric. A small group, commonly called a covendom, gathered at the New Earth Temple and suggested to Eric that he play up to Carla, David and me and infiltrate Jubilee Christian Center in order to expose all the hypocrisy they believed must exist there. The scheme sounded interesting to Eric and Sandra, but as Eric listened to and watched his friends, he began to discern anger on their faces and hear words that didn't represent the philosophy true followers of Wicca were supposed to believe. Where was the real hypocrisy here?

As he continued to listen intently to their elaborate plans for infiltration and spiritual espionage, Eric remembered the love the Christians had shown him. He began to feel guilty. A double agent for the pagans—what an idea! The whole thing began to sour in his insides.

It took a little creative doing, but we arranged for Eric and Sandra to attend our 11:00 a.m. service on Sunday, two weeks after the Halloween prayer meeting. The sanctuary was jam-packed. As many saw Eric arriving, an excitement hung in the air. "Could this be his day?" they wondered. "Who knows, maybe both of them will come to Jesus." The worship service was powerful and I preached a simple message on "God's Incentive Program." As I prepared to give the invitation, as I do every service, I could sense some people praying fervently in the Spirit. Hands began going up in response to the invitation all over the sanctuary. I looked at the front row where my special guest sat. Eric first glanced up at me with a look of surrender on his face, then shot up his hand. Sandra followed suit.

Nearly twenty souls made their way to the altar, among them the high priest of the New Earth Temple and his disciple Sandra. Goodbye, witchcraft; hello, Jesus! The place exploded in hallelujahs, cheers and tears. Moreover, it just so happened that Larry Lea had sent out a cameraman to interview several of us about the after-effects of the San Francisco Breakthrough, and on video tape he captured Eric and Sandra coming forward.

That afternoon we ate and fellowshiped with our new brother and sister. After the evening service we went over to Pastor David's house to view a television special we had taped earlier for secular distribution as a ministry to the unchurched. As 11:00 p.m. drew near, I felt exhausted. Carla wasn't through ministering to our two friends, so I excused myself and went home.

At approximately 3:00 a.m., I was awakened by my excited wife, "Well, they got the power!" she exclaimed.

"What?" I sleepily replied, teetering halfway between dreamland and reality.

"They were filled with the Holy Ghost and both speak in tongues!" she boldly shouted to her groggy husband. "If he's going to do what he said he's going to do, then he needs all the power he can get," she added with a note of concern.

"What is he going to do?" I asked.

"He's going to tear down the New Earth Temple with his own hands." By now I was wide awake. *I better get some advice on this one*, I thought.

Destroying Accursed Things

The timing of the Lord never ceases to amaze me. Earlier, Carla and I had made plans to have dinner with Ed and Ruth Silvoso. The Silvosos had just returned from Argentina, where for months the city of Resistencia had been under Christian siege. Working with the local pastors, Ed's ministry, called Harvest Evangelism, had laid out a plan to take the city house by house, block by block. Peter and Doris Wagner, Cindy Jacobs and a few hundred ministers, intercessors and lay people from the states were involved, along with the leading evangelists and pastors of Argentina.

Over dinner Ed and Ruth described how each night of the final crusade they would burn idols, fetishes and accursed objects that had intrinsic demon power. Some very strange things took place during these burnings. Sometimes evil spirits would scream out of their human hosts. Carla and I listened intently to these stories as we envisioned the occult objects in Eric's temple.

One incident Ed shared in great detail. One night a woman had begun convulsing and writhing like a snake. Carlos Annacondia, the powerful evangelist, had commanded the woman's human spirit to take control of her body. He then had asked her where the stronghold of this oppression lay. She had answered that it resided in a little bottle of perfume in her purse. Apparently this bottle and its contents had been dedicated to a spirit.

Hearing this, I remembered that in the book of Joshua the Israelites had been warned not to take anything dedicated to false gods lest they be cursed:

"And you, by all means keep yourselves from the accursed things, lest you become accursed when you take of the accursed things, and make the camp of Israel a curse, and trouble it. "

Joshua 6:18

Ed continued his story. The perfume bottle had been removed from the woman's purse and smashed. At that moment, the demonized woman had cried out, "Jesus, Jesus!" and been instantly freed.

Ed's story also pointed out the dangers of such deliverances. As the bottle was smashed, a small portion of perfume spilled on a bystander. The next evening this brother almost died. Coincidence? Perhaps not. More than likely he had been in fear as he watched all this taking place, and when the spirits were dislodged they looked for the first available darkness in a nearby human to latch onto.

As we ate dinner with Ed and Ruth, listening intently to these stories from Argentina, we shared about the San Francisco Breakthrough and what had happened with Eric Pryor. We told them that the next day Eric was determined to tear down the temple and its altars and burn everything. David Brimmer, Jubilee member Rick Camuso and I had agreed to assist Eric. Ed advised us to be very careful, to get up early and cleanse ourselves in prayer and to humble and judge ourselves of any sin. We did this and more as we prepared for this encounter.

Like Josiah in 2 Kings 23, we came full of zeal to destroy the altars. The New Earth Temple on Geary Street in San Francisco was located inside the Masonic Temple, a temple within a temple. Four altars representing the north, south, east and west along with other strange items stared back at us. The air was thick. David began coughing incessantly.

Let's get it over with, I thought.

Eric was in more of a hurry than the rest of us. We had brought a mini-cam to record this historic event, but the lights in the temple began flashing on and off. Eric reminded us that the spirits weren't at all happy about this frontal attack. Because it was dark outside, each time the lights went out we had to wait several minutes for their return before we could continue the dismantling process.

Eric's collection of crystals was impressive. He estimated their value at approximately $40,000 to $50,000, including two rare Brazilian crystal skulls. One horned mask on the wall was three hundred years old, he noted.

Eric tore everything down. The objects were destined to be burned and destroyed the following Sunday after church, just as in Acts 19:18-20.

And many who had believed came confessing and telling their deeds. Also, many of those who had practiced magic brought their books together and burned them in the sight of all. And they counted up the value of them, and it totaled fifty thousand pieces of silver. So the word of the Lord grew mightily and prevailed.

The next Thursday was Thanksgiving. As usual, Carla's family came to our house to feast on my wife's specialties. This Thanksgiving was extra-special, for we had two new guests, brother Eric Pryor and his soon-to-be wife, sister Sandra.

"But I say to you who hear: Love your enemies, do good to those who hate you, bless those who curse you, and pray for those who spitefully use you. To him who strikes you on the one cheek, offer the other also. And from him who takes away your cloak, do

not withhold your tunic either. Give to everyone who asks of you. And from him who takes away your goods do not ask them back. And just as you want men to do to you, you also do to them likewise. But if you love those who love you, what credit is that to you? For even sinners love those who love them. And if you do good to those who do good to you, what credit is that to you? For even sinners do the same. And if you lend to those from whom you hope to receive back, what credit is that to you? For even sinners lend to sinners to receive as much back. But love your enemies, do good, and lend, hoping for nothing in return; and your reward will be great, and you will be sons of the Highest. For He is kind to the unthankful and evil. Therefore be merciful, just as your Father also is merciful.

Luke 6:27-36

The curse was reversed!

Chapter 10

The World of the Neo-Pagan

The modern practitioners of ancient magical arts embrace many diverse methodologies. Here in the San Francisco Bay Area there are an estimated 50,000 believers and workers of the "craft." Most of these "pagans" do not want to be linked to the satanists. They, in fact, denounce the blatant evil energy that comes from that camp. They prefer to call themselves Druids, goddess worshipers, magi, followers of Wicca, and other neo-pagan titles. As Margot Adler wrote in her book *Drawing Down the Moon:*[1]

While Neo-Paganism and modern Wicca are very anarchistic religions and it is probably wrong to say all Pagans believe this or that, there are some basic beliefs that most people in this book share:

"The world is holy. Nature is holy. The body is holy. Sexuality is holy. The mind is holy. The imagination is holy. You are holy. A spiritual path that is not stagnant ultimately leads one to the understanding of one's own divine nature. Thou art Goddess. Thou art God. Divinity is imminent in all Nature. It is as much within you as without. In our culture which has for so long denied and denigrated the feminine as negative, evil or, at best, small and unimportant, women (and men too) will never understand their own creative strength and divine nature until they embrace the creative feminine, the source of inspiration, the Goddess within. While one can at times be cut off from experiencing the deep and ever present connection between oneself and the universe, there is no such thing as sin (unless it is simply defined as that estrangement) and guilt is never very useful. The energy you put into the world comes back."

The neo-pagans I have met are, for the most part, very gentle people. They see themselves as secular stewards of creation, truly concerned for planet Earth and its inhabitants. To satisfy their craving for spirituality they embrace this non-authoritarian, non-dogmatic approach to higher power. They call themselves "wise ones" and are proud of the fact that their beliefs date back far before the Christian era. The problem, of course, is that following these ideals apart from Jesus is a dead-end road. Paul addressed this in Romans 1:18-23:

For the wrath of God is revealed from heaven against all ungodliness and unrighteousness of men, who suppress the truth in unrighteousness, because what may be known of God is manifest in them, for

God has shown it to them. For since the creation of the world His invisible attributes are clearly seen, being understood by the things that are made, even His eternal power and Godhead, so that they are without excuse, because, although they knew God, they did not glorify Him as God, nor were thankful, but became futile in their thoughts, and their foolish hearts were darkened. Professing to be wise, they became fools, and changed the glory of the incorruptible God into an image made like corruptible man—and birds and four-footed beasts and creeping things.

Even though gentle by nature, these "seekers of truth," like all deceived people, fall prey to the roaring lion. The spirits they tap into are not, as they claim, "nature spirits," but demons—clever, manipulative and very destructive evil spirits.

Pagan Practices

Ritual constitutes a large part of pagan community activities. Altar arrangements, cauldron rites, the circle of divination, the eighth grove festivals, the going of the ways, rites for the dead and other terms are common jargon to the devoted. Meditation, rhythmic breathing, chanting, invocation and evocation are all necessary practices for the true follower. Carved candles of various colors with mystical meanings figure prominently in "projection." To the pagan, the astral plane holds real meaning, so if a candle is properly carved and lit with the use of a talisman, or charm, and invocation of specific desired goals, the spirit world will manifest itself back into the physical realm with corresponding results.

To override someone's will, such as in a matter of the heart, financial dealings or general bewitchment, certain shapes must be carved with added oils and incense. Prescriptions can get very detailed, and each point must be followed precisely or things can go awry. Symbols, crystals, the tarot and so forth also play significant roles in bringing about the desired result.

These practices may seem to some like silly parlor tricks or the reaction of adults taking Halloween too seriously, but the power is real and all around us. Even though most pagans stay clear of curse placing, plenty of others use black magic to target the downfall of Christians.

A minister who fell into sin and lost his family and his ministry told me he had come under the spell of a beautiful woman in his church. Reflecting on this tragedy, he became convinced she had had some supernatural help luring him into her web. He said he would be home reading his Bible and begin to feel her presence. He could hear her calling to him, even though she lived miles away. Of course, the man admitted he had been an easy target because of his poor relationship with his wife and because the pressures of pastoring were wearing him down. His big mistake was not getting counsel.

If you plan to do anything substantial for the Kingdom of God, make sure you know how to stand with the full armor of God intact.

For we do not wrestle against flesh and blood, but against principalities, against powers, against the rulers of the darkness of this age, against spiritual hosts of wickedness in the heavenly places.

Ephesians 6:12

Pagan Terminology

I think it would be useful for us to examine the nomenclature of people who use the black arts or crafts to curse others. Here in the States there is a growing community of people tapping into powers they don't fully understand. Referencing *The Donning International Encyclopedic Psychic Dictionary*,[2] let us look into the world of the occult.

Curse: to use an elemental for the transference of evil psychic energy; psychic intensifies mind activity by focusing on a thought-form until it is dense enough to mold into an elemental, into which he or she pours a part of themselves; this gives the elemental intelligence and connects it to her or him; psychic aims at a chosen object, person, or area they want to bring harm; the elemental thought-form is then invoked in the name of an activity and an entity; e.g., "I curse you, Bob, to break a bone," which endows the elemental with an independent life of its own; as long as the psychic keeps their mind activity on this elemental and keeps it solidified with anger and evil intentions, the elemental will hover over the head of the victim and bring its intent to pass; a curse employs no physical article, but is a product of inner tension of the psychic which is released in negativity; some psychics use a plant or animal in the victim's house from which substance is drawn to influence the victim [page 148].

Hex: (United States) to use black magic to harm another person's body, family, or property by means of deep concentration, rituals, and utilizing the law of mimicry and the law of contagion; bodily harm can show as marks on the neck, bruises on the body, odors coming from the victim, sexual impotence, breaking out in a sweat for no apparent reason, vomiting, pricking pains, kidney or stomach pains; property damage can result in fire, the smell of rotting flesh around the house, and animals getting sick or dying for no reason [page 281].

Spell: 1. a period of time during which a person or object is held captive by a psychic (usually for evil intent); one person can stimulate another person's brain while the victim is in the alpha state of consciousness; accomplished by thought transference accompanied by such strong emotions that the resistance of the nerve gap is reduced and the acetylcholine is undissolved; this breaks down one's resistance to another's message; emotion transferred is either extremely fearful or extremely pleasurable; in spelling, the eye-stare and emotionally planned ploy from one person puts another in the alpha state for susceptibility; period of spell can last through one encounter of twenty minutes to half a day or for many days; 2. a word, words, music, or a chant designed to have a dominating or irresistible influence over another individual; i.e., incantations, complimentary ploy. Usage: the spell of fine music. 3. to spell; to use one's eyes to stare at another individual, animal, or object for a period of time; energy is thus beamed from the eyes in an icy, destructive, fearful stare or in a pleasurable, enticing, lovable stare; either stare deprives the victim of the power of resistance [page 579].

Casting a Spell: to hold a person captive to the point that the victim experiences events and thoughts which they cannot account for; and yet feels that they are from his or her own personal effort; done by one of the following processes: 1. beaming energy out of the eyes: staring at the victim with intentional threat; the victim becomes fearful and transfixed, losing his or her resistance in anticipation that the speller will do something destructive; 2. beaming energy out of the eyes by using the eye-stare in the exact opposite manner: keeping the victim enthralled by the power of pleasing them, coming from deep within the eye-starer; delighting the victim to a high degree with tender loving ploy, making the victim easily held captive; 3. using special magic chants and songs that were written to weaken a person's will, and to allure the victim into an easily manipulated state of consciousness; this psychic skill can be used in reverse: to hold an individual captive for their protection, so they cannot be manipulated [page 97].

Magic: now also considered an art; 1. comprises a system of concepts and methods of using the more subtle forces of nature to help individuals balance with their emotions; teaches how to alter the electrochemical aspect of the body metabolism, using association techniques and objects to concentrate and focus the emotional energy; attempts to help one achieve a higher state of consciousness and improvements in environmental atmosphere; 2. develops control of human will; uses some alchemical procedures; 3. utilizes the psychic skills that use the energy emanating from one's body, adjusting it to interact with other energy patterns, animate or inanimate, according to one's will; 4. belief: the soul-mind lives on after physical death and can be called upon for help in the mundane world; uses techniques to conjure up their assistance; 5. uses incantations, ceremonies, symbols, nature objects, man-made objects, to simulate and therefore stimulate the more subtle forces to obey; relies on these two laws: (hermetic) "as above so below"; "respect nature and have control over it"; 6. two kinds: black magic used for evil intent; white magic used for righteous purposes; (do not confuse with high magic and low magic which are steps in white magic). Syn. Hidden science, great science, mysticism, parapsychology [page 366].

Charming: 1. energizing a talisman; to impregnate an article or object with psychic energy with the intent that it will bring good fortune to the owner; frequently performed by a priest in a special ritual. 2. exercising psychic energy to change the movement or action of a living organism, including humans, for a set length of time; an object that has been energized with cantations, chanting, rituals, etc., can be used. Syn. Casting a spell [page 107].

Active Ritual: involvement of direct discharge of energy from agent to target; to psychically discharge concentrated energy to the target [page 4].

Bewitching: to use one's psychic influence over another person for the purpose of manipulating his thoughts and actions; bewitcher uses beamed energy from an eye-stare, incantations, or rituals of magic to put his victim in a transfixed state; this beamed energy is either an icy, destructive, fearful stare or a pleasurable, enticing, lovable stare; verbiage and chants are accompanied appropriately; results in the victim experiencing events that cannot be attributed to his own personal efforts; sometimes the victim is unaware that his actions are not his own; lasts from a few hours to many years. Syn. Casting a spell. Syn. charming, enchanting, fascinating [page 65].

Enchant(ing): 1. to reach and invoke the etheric world intelligences by singing and chanting; songs and chants are composed with the proper rhythm, pitch, and tone to stir up vibrations in the atmosphere and prepare the conscious mind of the magician (to be passive and neutral) making etheric world communication easier. 2. to subject one to psychic energy; to impart a magic quality or effect in the atmosphere around a person, by intensified concentration of one's mind; e.g., (a) to physically concentrate on a patient, consistently, imparting healing energy into their aura until the patient shows much relief; (b) to psychically concentrate on a victim and send energy with evil intent until the victim is in an accident. Syn. charm, spell [page 204].

Isn't it amazing how many occultic words we use in our everyday language? "Charmed, I'm sure." "I was spellbound." "The movie was enchanting." "Our date was magic." I'm sure you can think of dozens more. Even though the Bible is very clear on the dangers of "idle words," we still lace our everyday conversations with unproductive sayings.

Death and life are in the power of the tongue, And those who love it will eat its fruit.

Proverbs 18:21

Endnotes

1. Beacon Press, 1979, p. ix.
2. By Juen G. Bletzer, Ph.D., Whitford Press, 1986.

Chapter 11

Issues and Answers from the Word

Some time ago a member of our church gave me a photocopy of a booklet called *Biblical Curses* put together by a pastor named Win Worley. This list of people or things that are cursed can be of great help in identifying sources of problems:

1. Those who curse or mistreat Jesus. (Deuteronomy 27:26; Genesis 27:29; Genesis 12:3; Numbers 24:9)

2. Those who are willing deceivers. (Joshua 9:23; Jeremiah 48:10; Malachi 1:14; Genesis 27:12)

3. An adulterous woman. (Numbers 5:27)

4. Disobedience to the Lord's Commandments. (Deuteronomy 11:28; Daniel 9:11; Jeremiah 11:3)

5. Idolatry. (Jeremiah 44:8; Deuteronomy 29:19; Exodus 20:5; Deuteronomy 5:8,9)

6. Those who keep or own cursed objects. (Deuteronomy 7:25; Joshua 6:18)

7. Those who refuse to come to the Lord's help. (Judges 5:23)

8. House of the wicked. (Proverbs 3:33)

9. He who gives not to the poor. (Proverbs 28:27)

10. The earth by reason of man's disobedience. (Isaiah 24:3-6)

11. Jerusalem is a curse to all nations if Jews rebel against God. (Jeremiah 26:6)

12. Thieves and those who swear falsely by the Lord's name. (Zechariah 5:4)

13. Ministers who fail to give the glory to God. (Malachi 2:2)

14. Those who rob God in tithes and offerings. (Malachi 3:9; Haggai 1:6-9)

15. Those who hearken unto their wives rather than God. (Genesis 3:17)

16. Those who lightly esteem their parents. (Deuteronomy 27:16)

17. Those who make graven images. (Deuteronomy 27:15; Exodus 20:4,5; Deuteronomy 5:8,9)

18. Those who willfully cheat people out of their property. (Deuteronomy 27:17)

19. Those who take advantage of the blind. (Deuteronomy 27:18)

20. Those who oppress strangers, widows or the fatherless (Deuteronomy 27:19; Exodus 22:22-24)

21. Him who lies with his father's wife. (Deuteronomy 27:20)

22. Him who lies with any beast. (Deuteronomy 27:21; Exodus 22:19)

23. Him who lies with his sister. (Deuteronomy 27:22)

24. Those who smite their neighbors secretly. (Deuteronomy 27:24)

25. Those who take money to slay the innocent. (Deuteronomy 27:25)

26. Adulterers. (Job 24:15-18)

27. The proud. (Psalm 119:21)

28. Those who trust in man and not in the Lord. (Jeremiah 17:5)

29. Those who do the work of the Lord deceitfully. (Jeremiah 48:10)

30. Him who keeps back his sword from blood. (Jeremiah 48:10; I Kings 20:35-42)

31. Those who reward evil for good. (Proverbs 17:13)

32. Illegitimate children. (Deuteronomy 23:2)

33. Children born from incestuous unions. (Genesis 19:36-38)

34. Murderers. (Exodus 21:12)

35. To murder indirectly. (Exodus 21:14)

36. Children who strike their parents. (Exodus 21:15)

37. Kidnappers. (Exodus 21:16; Deuteronomy 24:7)

38. Those who curse their parents. (Exodus 21:17)

39. Those who cause the unborn to die. (Exodus 21:22,23)

40. Those who do not prevent death. (Exodus 21:29)

41. Those involved in witchcraft. (Exodus 22:18)

42. Those who sacrifice to false gods. (Exodus 22:20)

43. Those who attempt to turn anyone away from the Lord. (Deuteronomy 13:6-9)

44. Those who follow horoscopes. (Deuteronomy 17:2-5)

45. Those who rebel against pastors. (Deuteronomy 17:12)

46. False prophets. (Deuteronomy 18:19-22)

47. Women who keep not their virginity until they are married. (Deuteronomy 22:13-21)

48. Adulterers. (Deuteronomy 22:22-27)

49. Parents who do not discipline their children, but honor them above God. (I Samuel 2:17, 27-36)

50. Those who curse their rulers. (I Kings 2:8,9; Exodus 22:28)

51. Those who teach rebellion against the Lord. (Jeremiah 28:16,17)

52. Those who refuse to warn them of sin. (Ezekiel 3:18-21)

53. Those who defile the sabbath. (Exodus 31:14; Numbers 15:32-36)

54. Those who sacrifice human beings. (Leviticus 20:2)

55. Participants in seances and fortune telling. (Leviticus 20:6)

56. Homosexual and lesbian relationships. (Leviticus 20:13)

57. Sexual intercourse during menstruation. (Leviticus 20:18)

58. Necromancers and fortune tellers. (Leviticus 20:27)

59. Those who blaspheme the Lord's name. (Leviticus 24:15,16)

60. Those who are carnally minded. (Romans 8:6)

61. Sodomy. (Genesis 19:13,24,25)

62. Rebellious children (Deuteronomy 21:18-21)[1]

If in this list you see an area you've violated, quickly repent, ask forgiveness and break free from its hold by renouncing your violation(s) by name. Apply the name of Jesus to it, and plead His blood to cleanse it. Here is a sample prayer for one who has had an abortion:

"Father, forgive me, for I have sinned. I have murdered an innocent child. I am sorry and I repent of my wicked deed. Lord, deliver me from the curse I have allowed to come into my life through this act. In Jesus' name, I break the powers of darkness over me and my children and my children's children. I cleanse my past with the blood of the Lamb, and from this day on, I walk in the light. Jesus has set me free this day from the curse. Amen and Amen..."

The Word as a Weapon

The Bible not only enlightens us about potential grounds for being cursed, but it also provides a powerful weapon for breaking the hold of such curses.

My son, give attention to my words;
Incline your ear to my sayings.
Do not let them depart from your eyes;
Keep them in the midst of your heart;

For they are life to those who find them,
And health to all their flesh.

Proverbs 4:20-22

Being schooled in the "Word" movement, I put a high premium on quoting specific scriptures for specific problems. I believe it is absolutely paramount when "binding and loosing" to quote the Word of God with "It is written..." With this in mind, let's find some profitable verses for dealing with potential curses. Again, when breaking a curse, name it and apply to it the name of Jesus, His blood and His Word. Here are a few scriptures for specific problems:

Alcoholism:	Joel 2:32
	Psalm 107:6
	II Corinthians 2:14
Uncontrollable anger:	Proverbs 16:32
	Proverbs 19:11
	Ephesians 4:31
Fear:	Philippians 4:6-7
	I Peter 5:7
Barrenness:	Deuteronomy 7:9-14
	Psalm 113:9
Blood disorders:	Proverbs 3:5-8
	Hebrews 4:12
	Joel 3:21
Cancer:	Proverbs 4:20-22
	III John 2
	James 5:16

Diseases in general:	Jeremiah 17:14
	Jeremiah 33:6
	Psalm 107:20
Disorders of the eyes and ears:	Isaiah 32:3
	Matthew 11:5
Insomnia:	Psalm 3:5
	Psalm 4:8
	Proverbs 3:24
Mental health:	Psalm 25:17
	Psalm 94:19
	Proverbs 16:3
Nervous disorders:	Psalm 46:1
	II Thessalonians 3:3
	Psalm 55:22
Poverty (financial problems):	Psalm 34:9-10
	Psalm 37:25
	II Corinthians 8:9

June Newman Davis has written a booklet that lists a wide variety of challenging situations and corresponding scriptures. This is a valuable little tool for locating answers for the problems we all face. For a copy of her booklet write to Scripture Key Ministries, P.O. Box 6559, Denver, Colorado 80206-0559.

The Christian's Greatest Defense

Christians who are walking in righteousness and holiness need have no fear of the enemy. While we wage mortal combat against him, our adversary may aim a barrage of curses at us like heavy artillery. But although we may take hits occasionally, no evil can take root in those who abide in Christ and in His Word. A curse has no defense against the Word!

"No weapon formed against you shall prosper, and every tongue which rises against you in judgment you shall condemn. This is the heritage of the servants of the Lord, and their righteousness is from Me," says the Lord.

Isaiah 54:17

Endnotes

1. *Curses and Soul Ties/Binding and Loosing Spirits*, by Win Worley, Booklet 5, 1983.